Supporting Gifted ELLs in the Latinx Community

This essential resource is designed to help your classroom, school, or district better identify and serve gifted English language learners in the Latinx community. Drawing on detailed case studies and vignettes from actual programs, chapters highlight the unique needs of gifted Latinx English language learners, and look at how you can best identify and support their development. Covering topics from teacher bias and systemic racism to best practices for engaging families and communities, this book lays out practical strategies and an accessible framework for implementing culturally responsive assessments, identification, and programming strategies.

Michelle Pacheco DuBois is the Gifted and Talented Coordinator for the Boulder Valley School District, Colorado, USA. She holds a Doctorate of Education in Curriculum and Instruction with a specialization in Gifted Education. Dr. DuBois teaches courses and conducts professional development in Colorado and around the country, focusing on culturally linguistically diverse and twice-exceptional learners. She has been awarded the Colorado Gifted Educator of the Year and recognized by the Colorado House of Representatives for her work with culturally linguistically diverse gifted learners.

Robin M. Greene is the Director of Gifted and Talented Education for Denver Public Schools, Colorado, USA. She holds a Doctorate of Education in Curriculum and Instruction with a specialization in gifted education. Dr. Greene is an international speaker who has presented workshops on culturally linguistically diverse gifted learners, culturally responsive gifted programming, and transformational leadership. She has published multiple articles on creativity and uses social justice and critical race theory to frame policies and practices for gifted learners.

Also Available from Routledge
Eye on Education
(www.routledge.com/k-12)

Sexuality for All Abilities: Teaching and Discussing Sexual Health in Special Education
Katie Thune and Molly Gage

Coding as a Playground: Programming and Computational Thinking in the Early Childhood Classroom, Second Edition
Marina Umaschi Bers

Culturally Responsive Self-Care Practices for Early Childhood Educators
Julie Nicholson, Priya Shimpi Driscoll, Julie Kurtz, Doménica Márquez, and LaWanda Wesley

Implementing Project Based Learning in Early Childhood: Overcoming Misconceptions and Reaching Success
Sara Lev, Amanda Clark, and Erin Starkey

Advocacy for Early Childhood Educators: Speaking Up for Your Students, Your Colleagues, and Yourself
Colleen Schmit

Grit, Resilience, and Motivation in Early Childhood: Practical Takeaways for Teachers
Lisa B. Fiore

Supporting Gifted ELLs in the Latinx Community

Practical Strategies, K–12

Michelle Pacheco DuBois and Robin M. Greene

NEW YORK AND LONDON

First published 2021
by Routledge
52 Vanderbilt Avenue, New York, NY 10017

and by Routledge
2 Park Square, Milton Park, Abingdon, Oxon OX14 4RN

Routledge is an imprint of the Taylor & Francis Group, an informa business

© 2021 Taylor & Francis

The right of Michelle Pacheco DuBois and Robin M. Greene to be identified as authors of this work has been asserted by them in accordance with sections 77 and 78 of the Copyright, Designs and Patents Act 1988.

All rights reserved. No part of this book may be reprinted or reproduced or utilised in any form or by any electronic, mechanical, or other means, now known or hereafter invented, including photocopying and recording, or in any information storage or retrieval system, without permission in writing from the publishers.

Trademark notice: Product or corporate names may be trademarks or registered trademarks, and are used only for identification and explanation without intent to infringe.

Library of Congress Cataloging-in-Publication Data
A catalog record for this title has been requested

ISBN: 978-0-367-46078-5 (hbk)
ISBN: 978-0-367-45693-1 (pbk)
ISBN: 978-1-003-02676-1 (ebk)

Typeset in Palatino
by Newgen Publishing UK

This book is dedicated to the families of gifted Latinx English language learners for your advocacy and passion in the pursuit of equitable access to gifted education and advanced programming for your children. It is also dedicated to those educators and administrators who are consistently striving to educate themselves and their communities by examining their own cultural bias and committing to challenging our educational systems for equity and excellence for ALL students.

Thank you to our families and your incredible support that has enabled us to pursue our passion. This would not be possible without you. To our patient and supportive partners, Casey and Robert, we thank you for supporting our endeavors and believing as strongly as we do that culturally and linguistically diverse gifted learners deserve equitable opportunity and access to advanced programming and culturally responsive gifted education. To our sons, Cameron and Benjamin, thank you for showing us all the good in the world and reflecting on our practices about the importance of leaving the world better than how we found it. Our message to you is to continue to embrace, recognize, and value the beauty of the diverse cultures in our world.

Contents

List of Figures viii

1 Overview and Introduction 1

2 Characteristics of Gifted Latinx Learners 20

3 Culturally Responsive Assessment Practices 34

4 Culturally Responsive Gifted Classrooms: Providing Access and Opportunity 61

5 Cultivating Culturally Responsive Gifted Professionals 86

6 The Critical Role of the Family and Community 97

7 Case Scenarios 107

8 Recommendations for Policy and Practice 130

Appendices 167

Figures

1.1 DuBois Greene Culturally Responsive Gifted Framework.........15
1.2 DuBois Greene Culturally Responsive Gifted Framework: Latinx ELLs.........16
2.1 Greene DuBois Latinx Gifted Behavior Observation Tool.........30
3.1 DuBois Greene Culturally Responsive Gifted Framework: Assessment.........35
3.2 Body of evidence.........36
3.3 Expanded body of evidence.........37
3.4 Student interview survey.........51
3.5 *Encuesta de entrevista estudiantes*.........52
4.1 DuBois Greene Culturally Responsive Gifted Framework: Programming.........62
4.2 Greene's Culturally Responsive Gifted Model.........66
5.1 DuBois Greene Culturally Responsive Gifted Framework: Professional Learning.........87
5.2 Strategic Plan for Developing Culturally Responsive Gifted Professionals.........88
6.1 DuBois Greene Culturally Responsive Gifted Framework: Family Engagement.........98
6.2 Family questionnaire.........103
6.3 *Cuestionario familiar*.........104
7.1 Body of evidence and programming plan.........108
8.1 DuBois Greene Culturally Responsive Gifted Framework: Latinx ELLs.........131
8.2 Professional learning roadmap.........152

1

Overview and Introduction

Overview

Supporting Gifted ELLs in the Latinx Community: Practical Strategies, K–12 has been written to support educators in their pursuit to identify and serve gifted English language learners who are Latinx. What is an English language learner? According to the U.S. Department of Education (2015), an

> English language learner is defined as an individual who has limited ability in speaking, reading, writing, or understanding of the English language, and whose native language is a language other than English; or who lives in a family or community environment where a language other than English is the dominant language.

English language learners are at risk of becoming dropouts, feeling frustrated, experiencing anxiety, and underachieving in school settings when they are misunderstood and assumptions are made about them by their teachers and administrators. The term "Latinx" refers to the gender-neutral version of Latino. Although the focus of this book is Latinx English language learners, much of the guidance can be applied to all English language learners. This book utilizes current research and best practices interlaced within the DuBois Greene Culturally Responsive Gifted Framework to provide recommendations for identification and programming for gifted Latinx English language learners.

The theme of culturally responsive gifted education (Ford, 2015; Ford & Moore, 2004; Greene, 2017) is woven throughout the book. An inclusive school system from policy to classroom practice that integrates the culture, norms, values, and experiences of gifted Latinx English learners while providing authentic and rigorous learning opportunities is imperative for learners to thrive. The authors detail the elements of identification, professional learning, instructional practices, policy review, and strategies needed to develop an inclusive culturally responsive gifted environment that is supportive of culturally different learners.

The early chapters of this book discuss the identification practices necessary for recruiting gifted Latinx English language learners, including an understanding of the barriers that impede identification. The chapters share the characteristics of gifted Latinx English language learners that may be overlooked based on outdated constructs of giftedness. These constructs, defined by the dominant culture's values and traits, have impacted the way giftedness is perceived. The early chapters of the book also include a deeper examination of the role of assessment in finding gifted Latinx English language learners, culturally fair assessments, and culturally responsive assessment practices that educators can adopt or add to their proverbial tool belt so as to allow for equitable access to programming.

The middle chapters of the book share the practices that are necessary to retain gifted Latinx English language learners, such as culturally responsive gifted programming, professional learning, and family engagement. Chapter 4 explores culturally responsive gifted programming by using Greene's Culturally Responsive Gifted Model (Greene, 2017), as a frame for understanding. Greene's Culturally Responsive Gifted Model is research based and blends culturally responsive education (including linguistically diverse education) and instructional practices with gifted education practices. It is this blend of practices that invites culturally different learners in (Ford, 2015) and leads to positive learner outcomes (Greene, 2017).

Chapter 5 explores the necessary prerequisite and essential understandings that are critical for developing culturally responsive gifted education professionals, including the impact and importance of a one's cultural identity, asset-based mindsets, culturally responsive education and gifted education as drivers for student success. In Chapter 6, the critical role of family and community engagement in identifying and serving gifted Latinx learners is explored.

The final chapters in the book explore how to sustain and strengthen culturally responsive gifted education. Incorporating the DuBois Greene Culturally Responsive Gifted Framework, Chapter 7 examines authentic case scenarios with recommendations for identification, programming, professional learning, and family engagement. The case scenarios are drawn from the authors' personal and professional experiences and highlight the strategies and programming necessary to support gifted Latinx English language learners. The scenarios are varied to demonstrate the broad differences among Latinx learners and their school and life experiences. The strategies shared examine the intersectionality of language, culture, and giftedness.

The book concludes with recommendations for policy and practices that may have a significant impact on the identification of and programming for gifted Latinx English language learners within school communities. In sum, this book has been written to heighten educators' awareness of gifted Latinx learners so that these learners are seen and identified, and receive access to gifted programming. By highlighting the assets and strengths of the gifted Latinx community, this content of this book aims to broaden the cultural lens of educators and interrupt a dominant culture perspective of gifted education, policies, and implementation of practices.

How to Use This Book

Supporting Gifted ELLs in the Latinx Community: Practical Strategies, K–12 is designed to guide educators in their quest to identify and program for gifted ELLs in a culturally responsive manner. This book can be used in a variety of ways that can be differentiated for the reader, based on their needs. One can choose to go through the book chapter by chapter and apply the components of the DuBois Greene Culturally Responsive Gifted Framework to develop guidance for gifted identification and programming protocols for gifted Latinx English language learners; alternatively, one can read the book in its entirety, examine current practices, then choose the individual chapters and guidance tools that will help refine practices.

With this book, educators at all academic levels, from prekindergarten to post-secondary, will learn strategies to guide the application of research-based best practices in gifted education, culturally responsive education, and linguistically diverse education, as well as how they connect to form the foundation of culturally responsive gifted education. *Supporting Gifted ELLs in the Latinx Community: Practical Strategies, K–12* is ideal to be used as a college textbook for those studying general education, gifted education, or culturally and linguistically diverse education and for those who are studying to be school and district-level administrators.

Although this book is written specifically for those working with gifted Latinx English language learners, many of the practices shared can be applied across diverse populations of learners. When reading through this book, should an educator find something applicable to other groups of learners, the authors would encourage the application across cultural groups.

Ultimately, this is a guide for all educational professionals who are invested in equitable gifted education and programming. It is for those who are determined to identify gifted Latinx English language learners, create culturally responsive gifted environments, grow in their practice and understanding of self, and lead for sustainable systemic change. In other words, *Supporting Gifted ELLs in the Latinx Community: Practical Strategies, K–12* is for those who are ready to interrupt white supremacy culture practices that perpetuate the underrepresentation of diverse learners in gifted and advanced programming such as Advanced Placement, International Baccalaureate, honors classes, and concurrent enrollment.

Introduction

Giftedness

To understand giftedness is to understand a very complex, and at times controversial, concept of neurodivergence in individuals. The early concepts of giftedness were rooted in racism through a myopic vision of intelligence that was focused on one particular demographic group: white affluent men of European descent. Early constructs of intelligence and concepts regarding potential can be traced back to the 1800s, with Sir Francis Galton the earliest researcher to report on human intelligence and intelligence testing. In 1905, Alfred Binet and Theodore Simon developed the first quantitative assessment of an intelligence construct that measured mental age to chronological age and brought forth the idea that children may be ahead of or behind the typical intellectual level for their actual age (Callahan & Hertberg-Davis, 2013). Binet saw intelligence is multifaceted and complex, consisting of both quantitative and qualitative components.

In 1916, Lewis Terman, known as the father of gifted education and a researcher at Stanford University, revised the Binet-Simon test to become the Stanford-Binet Intelligence Test and simplified the test greatly. Terman's refinement and development of the Stanford-Binet Intelligence Test simplified intelligence and influenced current understandings of an intelligence quotient, or IQ (Colangelo & Davis, 2003). Terman's research, based largely on his deep belief in eugenics (Maldonado, 2019), shaped the field of gifted education's constructs of how giftedness manifests and how intelligence is measured.

Terman believed that intelligence was an inherited trait that could be identified to "improve the human race" (Maldonado, 2019). He used the Stanford-Binet Intelligence Test to argue that the IQs of African American, Indigenous, and Latinx citizens were deficient, and therefore these groups of citizens were inferior to those of White European descent. (Maldonado, 2019; Terman, 1916). Terman's own racism shaped the study, the hypothesis, and the outcome. Unfortunately, that outcome shaped psychologists' and educators' views of who gifted learners were, and directly impacted policies and practices, for decades, thus institutionalizing racism in gifted education. In Terman's studies, those who were considered "geniuses" were individuals who demonstrated the characteristics of white supremacy culture, such as perfectionism, paternalism, and individualism; while some gifted children, across all cultures, do have traits such as perfectionism and a strong sense of individualism, this does not reflect either the dynamic intelligence or the cultural values of Latinx and Latinx English language learners.

In 1972, the first formal definition of gifted and talented was published by Congress in the Marland Report, defining gifted and talented as follows:

> Gifted and talented children are those identified by professionally qualified persons who by virtue of outstanding abilities are capable of high performance. These are children who require differentiated educational programs and services beyond those normally provided by the regular school program in order to realize their contribution to self and society. Children capable of high performance include those with demonstrated achievement and/or potential ability in any of the following areas: (a) general intellectual ability (GIA), (b) specific academic ability, (c) creative or productive thinking, (d) leadership ability, (e) visual and performing arts, (f) psychomotor ability. Children and youth with outstanding talent who perform or show the potential for performing at remarkably high levels of accomplishment when compared with others of their age, experience, or environment.
>
> (Marland, 1972)

In 1993, the U.S. Department of Education embraced a more diverse definition of gifted and talented by stating that, "Outstanding talents are present in children and youth from all cultural groups, across all economic strata, and in all areas of human endeavor" (U.S. Department of Education, 1993). Close to ten years later, the definition of gifted education aimed to describe the learner profile and or preferences of a student who was identified as gifted and talented. In 2002, under Title IX general provisions, and as a part of the federal Elementary and Secondary Education Act, gifted and talented was defined as

> students, children, or youth who give evidence of high achievement capability in areas such as intellectual, creative, artistic, or leadership capacity, or in specific academic fields, and who need services or activities not ordinarily provided by the school in order to fully develop those capabilities.
> (U.S. Department of Education, Title IX)

Neither the 1993 nor the 2002 definition of gifted learners included students with disabilities or linguistic diversity. However, gifted learners can have "learning and processing disorders that require specialized intervention and accommodation" (NAGC, 2020). Diversity within ability and language as well as race, class, and gender has made its way into many definitions of giftedness as the state and local level. (NAGC, 2020).

While numerous definitions of gifted and talented have been adopted by various groups in education, there is no singular definition that is embraced by everyone in the field of gifted education. This lack of cohesion, according to some scholars, can undermine gifted education as a whole. As Jim Delisle (2014, p. 13) states, "It is hard to serve these students well when we can't even agree on who they are." These multiple definitions can create confusion, and often do not explicitly name students of color. Because of multiple definitions and a lack of representation of culturally and linguistically diverse students, those in the field of gifted education find themselves continually advocating for the need for programming (Delisle, 2014).

Many of the definitions of giftedness have common language, including terms such as "outstanding talent," "high academic performance," and "potential"; none of the definitions include the terms "bilingualism" or "bilingual language abilities" (Valdés, 2003). Valdés (2003) reviewed gifted and talented literature in her research and reported that only Gardner's theory of multiple intelligences mentions linguistic intelligence, although even this is from a monolingual perspective. Valdés suggests that the current definitions of gifted and talented should be extended to include bilingual abilities and that the field of gifted education must embrace bilingualism as a strength of many gifted Latinx English language learners. More often than not, Latinx English language learners are overlooked for gifted programs and advanced programming opportunities due to limited English skills. Many educators and administrators believe that only when a student is fluent in English can they then be referred for gifted programming and offered advanced academic opportunities. This practice continues to exacerbate the exclusion from and access to gifted programming for Latinx learners.

Since 2002, the U.S. Department of Education's Office of Civil Rights has been collecting gifted student data from U.S. school districts (Office of Civil Rights, 2020). Year after year, these data reflect the underrepresentation of Latinx learners in gifted education. A recent national report entitled *System Failure: Access Denied* (Gentry, Gray, Whiting, Maeda, & Pereira, 2019) found that although Latinx students have equal access to gifted identification processes, they remain underrepresented in gifted programs. The study does not, however, discuss Latinx English language learners and the role played by language acquisition and English proficiency in identification and programming.

As gifted programs become more inclusive, educational professionals should remember that equitable and equal access to gifted programming is expected to occur, regardless of language proficiency. In 2013, the legal case *McFadden v. Board of Education for Illinois School District U-46* was one of the first Office of Civil Rights complaints against gifted education for intentional linguistic and racial discrimination (Ford, 2014). In this case, the school district was found guilty of intentionally segregating its gifted programming based on language proficiency. When students became proficient in English, often the students weren't able to transfer into another gifted program because there was a different set of criteria for host-language peers. The court ultimately ruled that District U-46 instead chose to

> separate gifted Hispanic students from their white peers, thus perpetuating the cultural distinctions and

barriers to assimilation that our nation's civil rights laws are dedicated to prevent. That this segregation occurs at the stage of a child's education and life when he is most vulnerable to identifying his opportunities by cultural differences only aggravates an otherwise disparate impact on these children.
(McFadden v. Board of Education for Illinois School District U-46, 2014)

Systemic barriers in education continue to be maintained, perpetuating the exclusion of gifted Latinx learners from gifted identification and access to advanced programming. These barriers range from implicit bias, assessments, and language acquisition to narrow concepts of giftedness. The following section examines these barriers and their implications for gifted Latinx learners.

Systemic Barriers

Implicit Bias

Hammond (2014) defines implicit bias as the unconscious attitudes and stereotypes that shape our responses to certain groups. Implicit bias is an involuntary attitude based upon a person's life experiences. Within the constructs of their own implicit bias, educators perceive students based upon their background knowledge and cultural experiences. When educators are unaware of their own implicit bias, this can affect gifted identification and advanced programming for gifted Latinx learners (Greene, 2017).

The consequences of an educator's implicit bias, mindsets, and misperceptions of gifted culturally linguistically diverse students have been well documented, and those misperceptions have a direct impact on teacher nominations and referrals to gifted programming, leading to underrepresentation in programming (Olszewski-Kubilius & Clarenbach, 2012). The construct from which they view intelligence may be impacted by their implicit bias, and may narrow their lens on the depiction of a gifted student. The teacher referral process contributes significantly to the underrepresentation of culturally and linguistically diverse students in gifted education. Intentionally or unintentionally, teacher referrals serve as gatekeepers for access to advanced programming and gifted identification for Latinx learners.

Assessments

Historically, standardized tests frequently used for gifted identification have been culturally biased against those students with limited English language proficiency as these tests are really a measure of conformity to middle-class academic values and achievement (Castellano, 2002). Traditionally, quantitative data has been the primary data used in gifted identification, thus minimizing the need for qualitative data. When quantitative data is the only data used in a gifted identification process, it limits access to gifted programming for Latinx English language learners. A review of assessments that the authors have found to be successful in the identification of gifted Latinx English language learners will be explored further in Chapter 3.

Perceptions of Language Proficiency

"One does not have to speak English in order to be gifted or academically talented" (Castellano, 2002). The statement by Castellano is a fundamental belief of the authors; however, it is not a universally internalized understanding by educators nominating learners for a gifted program. Often students with limited English proficiency are not referred for gifted programming because of educator perceptions and expectations of Latinx English language learners (Castellano, 2002; Kogan, 2001). Unfortunately, many educators associate linguistic ability and language proficiency in the host language (English) with intellectual ability.

The road to language proficiency, however, is complex and involves multiple physiological changes within the brain, including the development of new cortical systems (Kennedy, 2006). During these changes, learners' acquisition of language, including understanding the architecture of language can develop at different rates. Educators without a basic understanding of individual differences in language acquisition may have misperceptions of ability and have a more difficult time identifying giftedness. Kogan (2001, p. 30) notes that educators may make judgments of students' abilities based on their perception of a learner's proficiency in English, use of non-standard English, use of Spanglish (when Spanish and English words, expressions, and phrases are used together in speech), or accent.

These gifted Latinx English language learners do indeed have linguistic abilities, but these are in their heritage (first) language. The antiquated idea that students should not be referred for gifted programming until they are fluent in English hinders access to advanced programming for Latinx learners. Limited English language proficiency should not be a barrier to gifted identification or advanced programming for Latinx learners. As mentioned previously, the *McFadden v. Board of Education for Illinois School District U-46* case did not rule in favor of the school district that was operating different programs based on language proficiency and race. The case is a reminder to all administrators and education professionals that the goal is not to make the learner fit the program; rather, the program should be modified to fit the learner.

Narrowed Concepts of Giftedness

The historical definition of giftedness by Terman (1926) proposes that giftedness resides within the top 1% of the population as measured by a high IQ score (Valdés, 2003). Terman's definition, rooted in racism, not only limits the area of gifted identification to one narrow concept of general intellectual ability, but discounts the cultural, linguistic, and social attributes of Latinx learners and other culturally and linguistically diverse learners. This narrow understanding of giftedness served as the foundation for the constructs of giftedness that continue to permeate and influence the field as a whole. Even Leta Hollingworth (1942), the forebear of gifted education, used Terman's Stanford-Binet Intelligence Scale to identify and study students who had IQs of 180 or higher and were identified as profoundly gifted. While she believed that giftedness could be found across races, and that all races should be included in gifted education, her studies reinforced the racist and classist underpinnings of gifted education that gifted learners are primarily white and middle-class.

Regardless of language acquisition and proficiency in English, Terman's and Hollingworth's understanding of giftedness is incredibly limited in its scope. As shared earlier, the field of gifted education continues to evolve in its understanding of how giftedness is represented across cultures. The field has recognized that the definitions of giftedness must be more inclusive, and that it needs to allow for cultural and linguistic diversity. Valdés (2003) suggests that a definition for gifted should include bilingual language abilities and interpreter competencies. Based on her research on bilingualism and young Latinx interpreters, Valdés (2003, p. 193) advocates for law-makers and policy-makers to include an additional area of giftedness: linguistic/analytic giftedness. According to Valdés, gifted Latinx English language learners who are identified with linguistic and analytic giftedness display the following characteristics:

- abstract and logical thinking
- an ability to store and retrieve information rapidly, accurately and selectively
- an ability to deal with complex problems
- adaptation to novel situations
- excellent memory
- high performance ability in communication
- high performance ability in interpersonal relationships
- sensitivity to the feelings of others.

The National Association for Gifted Children's definition states that gifted children, "Come from all racial, ethnic, and cultural populations, as well as all economic strata," thus supporting the view that Latinx students, as well as Latinx English language learners, can be gifted (NAGC, (2020). Expanding the definition of gifted can help to broaden teacher's perceptions of what gifted looks like among various cultural groups, in order to be more inclusive. Consequently, this has the power to increase access for gifted Latinx learners to advanced programming.

Systemic Racism

Keith Lawrence and Terry Kehler (2004, p. 1) define systemic and structural racism as

> the normalization and legitimization of an array of dynamics—historical, cultural, institutional and interpersonal—that routinely advantage whites while producing cumulative and chronic adverse outcomes for people of color. It is a system of hierarchy and inequity, primarily characterized by white supremacy—the preferential treatment, privilege and power for white people at the expense of Black, Latino, Asian, Pacific Islander, Native American, Arab and other racially oppressed people.

Systemic and structural racism permeates history, politics, and economics, and is enmeshed in society. Institutional racism is an offspring of systemic and structural racism that occurs within an organization such as the larger education system, as well as between different school systems. Institutional racism is found in the policies created, practices implemented, and inequitable opportunities and access to programming reinforced on the basis of race, language, or culture.

Considering gifted education's past, its early researchers' support of eugenics, and its roots of exclusionary practices, gifted education has a long history with systemic, structural, and institutionalized racism. These forms of racism are another barrier for gifted Latinx English language learners on their path to being identified and receiving gifted and talented programming. The policies created by the state or local school district can perpetuate institutional, systemic, and structural racism because of factors such as identification protocols, assessment requirements, programming requirements, and how the educators interact with families and the types of family engagement opportunities they create, which are culturally and linguistically responsive.

A deeper look into individual school district practices can show how institutionalized racism is reinforced. With more students being identified once they have been redesignated as proficient in English, there should be an examination of the district's assessment tools and assessment practices. The decisions to use certain assessments or specific practices can help to reinforce the narrative that English language learners are not gifted.

Cultural Responsiveness

One antidote to the insidiousness of systemic and institutionalized racism within gifted education is for education professionals to embrace culturally responsive pedagogy teaching. A culturally responsive educator forms relationships and values the culture of the learners in their classroom. The culturally responsive educator understands that the instructional practices, classroom experiences, and school environment must be inclusive, and that they need to embody and represent the lived experiences of racially, ethnically, and linguistically diverse learners (Gay, 2010, 2018; Ladson-Billings, 1995).

The act of being a culturally responsive educator is also done with intention. It involves developing a deeper understanding of the student's culture beyond surface-level clichés of holidays, heroes, and food. When an educator is able to understand a student's prior experiences, the values and belief systems that operate within cultures (frames of reference), and the manifestation and representation of culture as it pertains to students accessing learning, they can make learning relevant, authentic, and sustainable. In other words, the educator "teaches *to* and *through*" (Gay, 2010, 2018) racially, ethnically, and linguistically diverse students.

DuBois Greene Culturally Responsive Gifted Framework

In working with the Latinx population, there are questions that we can ask ourselves: How can we course-correct and disrupt a system that for several hundred years has benefited one group of individuals across the globe? How do we see heritage language for the value that it is and not a deficit? How does one see something through a lens that is not theirs? How do we take the work of scholars, theorists, and practitioners to create major paradigm shifts in thinking and behaviors so that gifted Latinx learners are able to be successful by design? These questions are a problem of practice for gifted education and one that concerns the authors of this book. The authors hope that their Culturally Responsive Gifted Framework can serve as a guide and inspire educators to make changes in identification and programming practices for gifted Latinx learners. The DuBois Greene Culturally Responsive Gifted Framework is designed to support the identification and programming of gifted culturally and linguistically diverse learners while incorporating equitable and culturally responsive practices. The DuBois Greene Culturally Responsive Gifted Framework is depicted in Figure 1.1 and Appendix A.

The Framework can be used with any culturally and diverse population; however, in this book the authors have used the Framework to specifically focus on gifted Latinx English language learners. The DuBois Greene Culturally Responsive Gifted Framework for gifted Latinx English language learners is depicted in Figure 1.2 and Appendix B.

The Framework has four components: assessment; programming; professional learning; and family engagement. These provide the basis for creating culturally responsive and equitable practices for gifted Latinx learners. Assessments are often one of the gatekeepers in the identification of

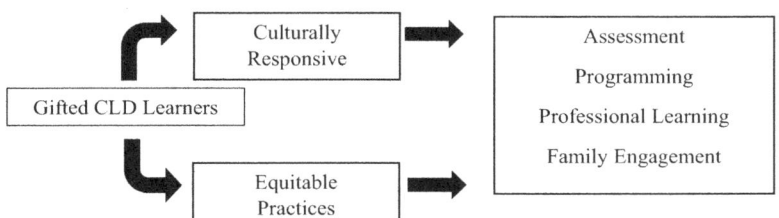

FIGURE 1.1
DuBois Greene Culturally Responsive Gifted Framework

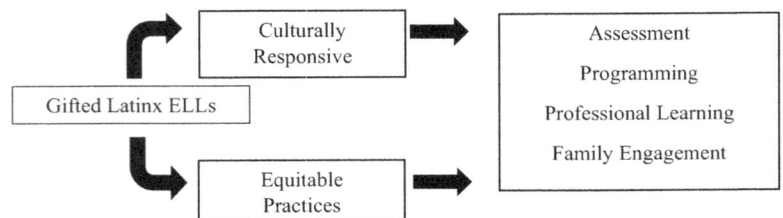

FIGURE 1.2
DuBois Greene Culturally Responsive Gifted Framework: Latinx ELLs

marginalized student populations. Many of the assessments used in gifted identification practices are designed with the majority culture in mind. They are generally not culturally or linguistically tailored toward Latinx students. Gifted and advanced programming opportunities are often not accessible to students unless they have been identified as gifted or until they are fluent in the English language. Teachers are generally one of the main referral points for students nominated for gifted education. Professional learning is one way teachers can be given training to recognize gifted students who are culturally and linguistically diverse. Families also need to be provided with opportunities to attend training focusing on gifted characteristics and programming for gifted Latinx learners. Each of the components will be examined in detail in the following chapters to guide educators in how they can utilize the Framework to increase identification and programming for gifted Latinx English language learners.

Key Points

- ♦ Historically, Latinx English language learners have been underrepresented in gifted programs in the United States.
- ♦ Culturally responsive means developing a deeper understanding of a student's culture beyond surface level clichés of holidays, heroes, and food.
- ♦ There is no single definition of "gifted" that is embraced by all in the field of gifted education.

- Current definitions of "gifted" do not include the terms "bilingualism" or "bilingual language abilities."
- Language should not be a barrier for access to gifted or advanced programming opportunities for Latinx English language learners.
- Systemic barriers perpetuate the exclusion of gifted Latinx English language learners from gifted identification and access to advanced programming range from implicit bias, assessments, language acquisition, and narrow concepts of giftedness.

References

Callahan, C., & Hertberg-Davis, H. (Eds.) (2013). *Fundamentals of gifted education: Considering multiple perspectives.* London: Taylor & Francis.

Castellano, J. A. (2002). Renavigating the waters: The identification and assessment of culturally and linguistically diverse students for gifted and talented education. In J. A. Castellano, & E. I. Dìaz (Eds.), *Reaching new horizons: Gifted and talented education for culturally and linguistically diverse students* (pp. 94–116). Boston: Allyn and Bacon.

Colangelo, N., & Davis, G. A. (2003). *Handbook of gifted education* (3rd ed.). Boston: Pearson Education.

Delisle, J. (2014). *Dumbing down America: The war on our nation's brightest young minds (and what we can do to fight back).* Waco, TX: Prufrock Press.

Ford, D. Y. (2014). School District U-46: A clarion call to school districts, state departments of education, and multicultural issues: Gifted education discrimination in *McFadden v. Board of Education for Illinois. Gifted Child Today, 37*(3), 188–193.

Ford, D. Y. (2015). Culturally responsive gifted classrooms for culturally different students: A focus on invitational learning. *Gifted Child Today, 38*(1), 67–69.

Ford, D. Y., & Moore J. L. III (2004). Creating culturally responsive gifted education classrooms: "Culture" is the first step. *Gifted Child Today, 27*(4), 34–39.

Gay, G. (2010). *Culturally responsive teaching*. New York: Teachers College Press.

Gay, G. (2018). *Culturally responsive teaching: Theory, research, and practice*. New York: Teachers College Press.

Gentry, M., Gray, A. M., Whiting, G. W, Maeda, Y., & Pereira, N. (2019). *System failure: Access denied*. West Lafayette, IN: Purdue University.

Greene, R. M. (2017). *Gifted culturally linguistically diverse learners: A school-based exploration* (Unpublished doctoral dissertation). University of Denver, Denver, CO.

Hammond, Z. (2014). *Culturally responsive teaching and the brain: Promoting authentic engagement and rigor among culturally and linguistically diverse students*. Thousand Oaks, CA: Corwin Press.

Hollingworth, L. S. (1942). Children above 180 IQ (Stanford-Binet). New York: World Book Company.

Kennedy, T. J. (2006). Language learning and its impact on the brain: Connecting language learning with the mind through content-based instruction. *Foreign Language Annals, 39*(3), 471–486.

Kogan, E. (2001). *Gifted bilingual students: A paradox?* New York: Peter Lang.

Ladson-Billings, G. (1995). Toward a theory of culturally relevant pedagogy. *American Educational Research Journal, 32*(3), 465–491.

Lawrence, K., & Keleher, T. (2004, November). Chronic disparity: Strong and pervasive evidence of racial inequalities: Poverty outcomes: Structural racism. Paper presented to For the Race and Public Policy Conference. Retrieved December 21, 2020, from www.intergroupresources.com/rc/Definitions%20of%20Racism.pdf

Maldonado, B. (2019, November 5). Eugenics on the farm: Lewis Terman. *The Stanford Daily*. Retrieved December 21, 2020, from www.stanforddaily.com/2019/11/06/eugenics-on-the-farm-lewis-terman

Office of Civil Rights. (2020). Civil rights data collection. Retrieved December 21, 2020, from https://https://ocrdata.ed.gov

Marland, S. P. (1972). *Education of the gifted and talented*. Report to the Congress of the United States by the U.S. Commissioner of Education. Washington, DC: U.S. Government Printing Office..

McFadden v. Board of Educ. for Illinois School Dist. U-46, 984 F.Supp.2d 882 (2013).

NAGC. (2020). About NAGC. Retrieved December 21, 2020, from www.nagc.org

Olszewski-Kubilius, P., & Clarenbach, J. (2012). *Unlocking emergent talent: Supporting high achievement of low-income, high-ability students*. Washington, DC: National Association for Gifted Children. Retrieved December 21, 2020, from https://files.eric.ed.gov/fulltext/ED537321.pdf

Terman, L. M. (1916). *The measurement of intelligence: An explanation of and a complete guide for the use of the Stanford revision and extension of the Binet-Simon Intelligence Scale*. Boston, MA: Houghton Mifflin.

Terman, L. M. (1926). *Genetic studies of genius: Vol. 1*. Palo Alto, CA: Stanford University Press.

U.S. Department of Education. (1993). *National excellence: A case for developing America's talent*. Washington, DC: U.S. Government.

U.S. Department of Education. (2015). *Title IX*. Retrieved December 21, 2020, from www.ed.gov/category/keyword/title-ix

Valdés, G. (2003). *Expanding definitions of giftedness: The case of young interpreters from immigrant communities*. London: Lawrence Erlbaum.

2

Characteristics of Gifted Latinx Learners

Latinx

The term "Latinx" was selected to represent the students in this book because of the term's inclusivity of all genders and sexual orientations of Latinos. Latinx learners are those students currently living in the United States and those born in or who have ancestors from Latin American countries, including the Caribbean, and Central and South America. In the United States, "Latino" is often conflated with the term "Hispanic"; however, not all Latinx learners are Hispanic because they may not speak Spanish. Put simply, Hispanic refers to a language spoken, while Latin America refers to geography. With this in mind, Latin America is incredibly diverse in both language and culture. With 33 countries comprising this part of the world, and over 400 languages spoken, how could it not be?

The Latinx population is the fastest growing population in the United States. The U.S. Latinx population reached a record 59.9 million in 2018, up from 47.8 million in 2008, according to the most recent U.S. Census Bureau population estimates (Flores, Lopez, & Krogstad, 2019). By 2060, Latinos are projected to represent 39% of the U.S. population under the age of five, compared with whites (31%), African Americans (13%), and Asians (7%) (U.S. Census Bureau, 2012).

The demographics of the United States are changing rapidly, with the Latinx population making up the majority population of our classrooms and forcing a shift in culture in our schools. Even with the changing demographics, there are still large gaps in academic achievement among Latinx learners and inequitable access to gifted education for these students. Gifted Latinx students have been overlooked for gifted identification and programming for over two decades.

It is important to note that there are different groups of students within the Latinx population: those who were born outside the United States to parents also born outside the United States, students who were born in the United States to parents born outside the United States, and students who are second-generation U.S. citizens, born to parents who were born in the United States to parents born outside of the United States. These students all come with a variety of experiences and knowledge as they strive for success in the school setting. Often children of immigrant families are challenged with navigating the majority culture without losing their heritage culture and language. Over the generations of being in the United States, the linguistic value placed upon the heritage language within a family often undergoes a metamorphosis, during which English becomes the valued language. When educators and administrators emphasize the importance of a student's heritage language in the school setting, students and families feel supported and respected by their school communities. The recognition and embracing of students' cultures helps to build strong relationships and foster respectful links with families.

Characteristics of Gifted Latinx English Language Learners

So why do Latinx learners continue to be underrepresented in gifted education? One reason is that gifted characteristics of Latinx students may display differently from those of non-Latinx students, depending on their background knowledge, access to learning opportunities, and cultural experiences. For example, in Latino cultures it is unseemly for individuals to draw attention to themselves. The cultural norm is that one is expected to be humble and not show off one's academic abilities. This is different from the majority culture, in which one is expected to rise to the top and show off one's abilities. Often the students who are nominated for gifted services by teachers are those who are predominantly the most noticeable in the classroom. Therefore, it is important that educators look at each individual in comparison with their cultural peers for characteristics that might indicate giftedness. The following characteristics have most commonly been observed by the authors among gifted Latinx learners.

Bilingualism

The term "bilingual" is defined as a person who is able to speak in two or more languages. That sounds relatively simple, but bilingualism is actually much more complex than that. What does it mean to be bilingual? To what extent does one need to speak in two or more languages to be considered a bilingual individual? As well as being able to speak in two or more languages, does being bilingual also include the domains of reading, writing, and listening? There are varying degrees of bilingualism and a continuum of proficiency levels.

In the school setting, English language proficiency levels of English language learners are generally measured using the four domains of academic language, which are speaking, listening, reading and writing (WIDA, 2014). Language development is dependent on multiple factors, including student personality, language exposure, instructional design, service delivery, scaffolding, and models for language (WIDA, 2014). Bilingually gifted students often demonstrate a high level of verbal ability in their heritage language, acquire the English language at a rapid pace, are interpreters, and have the ability to code switch.

High Verbal Ability in Heritage Language

Historically, English has been the primary language taught in U.S. public schools. When students come to school they come with their heritage language. In the case of Latinx learners, the language primarily spoken is Spanish, which is often devalued as a language when it is a student's native language. Ironically, when Spanish is learned as a second language by a white student, the value of the language increases. The design of the educational system promotes assimilation into the majority culture, which often eliminates students' use of their heritage language and a connection to their native culture.

Many gifted Latinx English language learners have a high level of verbal ability in their heritage language. These students have extensive vocabularies and are able to clearly express their thoughts and ideas in their native language. Gifted Latinx learners with high verbal ability often read at two or more grade levels above in their heritage language (Castellano & Frazier, 2011). It is important for educators to understand language as a right for students; this refers to individuals' rights to speak in and preserve their heritage language (Macías, 2016). A student's heritage language should not be diminished as less valuable than English, but rather should be honored and respected for its important role in students' lives.

Rapid Acquisition of English

Many gifted Latinx English language learners with high verbal ability in their heritage language quickly acquire English. This rapid acquisition of English is an indicator that a Latinx student might be a bilingually gifted student. Granada (2003) distinguishes the bilingual gifted student as one who primarily demonstrates giftedness linguistically whereas a gifted bilingual student is a student who is bilingual but demonstrates giftedness in different areas other than the linguistic field.

The bilingual gifted student is one who masters English within half the time compared with their native language peers. These students come to school speaking their heritage language and exit out of an English Second Language program within two to three years of entering the program or grow more than two levels in one year's time, as measured by assessments of language proficiency. This is twice the expected rate of learning for a typical English language learner, as a typical rate is five to six years (WIDA, 2014).

Interpreter

In this context, the term "interpreter" refers to a student's oral interpretation of language. Interpreting is a complex cognitive process involving analysis, synthesis and revision within three areas of operation: syntactic, semantic, and pragmatic, which co-occur with the stages of parsing, expression, development, ideation, and planning (Valdés, 2003). Valdés (2003) explains that interpreters must be able to retrieve words quickly, repeat a message while listening simultaneously, remember what was said, and reflect on language structure and the meaning it conveys. There are varying levels of interpreters spanning from rudimentary to a high level of interpretation.

Many bilingual gifted Latinx English language learners are capable of high-level interpretation skills. These gifted Latinx learners are often interpreters for their parents and classroom peers when they need assistance in communicating with monolingual English speakers. Interpreters are able to adapt their tone, style, and register to the demands of the interaction and social context (Valdés, 2003). The authors are not suggesting that all Latinx learners who demonstrate the ability to interpret are gifted, but that those students who do demonstrate superior interpreter abilities should have them documented as evidence for potential gifted identification.

Code Switching

Code switching is a complex phenomenon that demonstrates the ability to alternate between two or more languages as well as modify and adapt one's register, tone, and affect based on the audience and environment. In order to code switch effectively, a student must possess a high level of understanding of the multiple cultures, as well as a deep understanding of the underlying structures and purposes of multiple language systems (Hughes, Shaunessy, Brice, Ratliff, & McHatton, 2006). There are multiple reasons why a student might code switch, such as trying to fit into a group or environmental situation. Code switching can be a social, cultural, or linguistic tool that allows students to integrate their experiences of two languages and two cultures into a cohesive whole (Hughes et al. (2006). Latinx students who have the ability to code switch may demonstrate higher intellectual metalinguistic capacity.

Easily Navigates Between Cultures

The term "culture" refers to the beliefs, values and customs common to a group of people. Culture is a learned process that begins after birth, based on the environment that surrounds someone. Understanding the nuances and learning the rules of the majority culture can be challenging for English language learners. However, gifted Latinx learners are more likely to be able to traverse with a greater ease between their native culture and that of the majority.

One of the cultural differences between the majority culture and the Latinx culture is the concept of collectivism and individualism. The Latinx culture is community centered, and is rooted in collectivism. Latinx students enjoy working in groups and discussing ideas openly among themselves to construct meaning or solve problems, whereas U.S. culture places an important emphasis on individualism and striving to work independently. In a typical classroom setting, this difference in approaches to work may lead to a cultural mismatch in which teachers with a dominant culture perspective may view Latinx learners as being disruptive or lazy. When in a group of native Latinx peers, it may appear as if these students are not completing their assignments or not taking their class work seriously, whereas in reality they are working together and sharing ideas openly as they complete the work given. The gifted Latinx learner may be distinct in these groups as the student who is asking insightful questions, leading the group discussion, and actively involved in their own learning as well as guiding the learning of the members in the group. These learners are able to adapt to the majority culture's behaviors and mannerisms in the classroom while preserving their own cultural norms. They are often recognized by others as a student who has the ability to make it in the Anglo-dominated society (Bernal, 1978, as cited in Castellano, 1998).

Creativity

Gifted Latinx English language learners can be highly creative in a variety of ways and genres. These students possess multiple perspectives associated with being bicultural and have exceptional mental processes associated with dual language capabilities (Granada, 2003). Gifted Latinx English language learners may exhibit rich imagery in writing and oral storytelling (Irby & Lara-Alecio, 1996). Their writing may include elements of their native culture and family stories that have been passed down from generation to generation.

Creative thinkers are risk-takers, much like individuals who are learning a new language, taking risks in written and verbal form (Castellano & Robertson, 2014). Learning a new language places students in a state of vulnerability in a school setting. These students are in an environment where they are taking daily risks in learning a new language and the social constructs that go with it.

Creativity can also be expressed through movement and dance. These behaviors might be observed during school or in after-school enrichment opportunities such as ballet folklórico or the school talent show. Gifted Latinx English language learners might also display creativity through movement within their own community. This could be demonstrated in a break dancing class at the local recreation center or dancing opportunities at the local church.

Advanced Sense of Humor

Gifted Latinx learners may also demonstrate high verbal ability by exhibiting a rich sense of humor (Irby & Lara-Alecio, 1996). They understand jokes and puns about cultural differences. Often these students do not find their peers' age-appropriate jokes funny, but express humor beyond that of age-peers and often have an adult sense of humor. Humor might also be displayed in the form of sarcasm.

Mathematical Ability

Gifted Latinx English language learners who are strong in mathematical abilities are able to see relationships and make connections faster than their peers. They are able to creatively problem-solve and understand a variety of ways to explain mathematical computations. Research shows that those students with bilingual brains have better creative problem-solving and visual spatial abilities which can manifest mathematically (Marian & Shook, 2012).

Gifted mathematical ability in Latinx students may take longer to detect when there is a language component involved and instruction is in English only. However, when determining high mathematical potential among Latinx learners, it is important to focus on talent development in the early years, such as kindergarten and first grade. Talent development is a framework in which students are provided with access to advanced programming and psychosocial skills (motivation, independence, growth mindset) that support them in a long-term continued path of achievement (Olszewski-Kubilius & Thompson, 2015). The idea that ability is malleable at early stages of development is the key concept of talent development. By placing high-potential math Latinx students into advanced math groups at an early age, an environment is provided in which students are exposed to high-level problem-solving skills and creative inquiry that they might not otherwise have had the opportunity to experience due to language bias. Students do not need to be identified as gifted or speak English fluently to benefit from this type of programming. Over time, the students with high levels of mathematical ability will emerge as their skills are naturally developed in a challenging environment.

Leadership

Outstanding leadership abilities are frequently demonstrated by gifted Latinx English language learners. These abilities can be seen in multiple settings and can manifest in a variety of ways. Leadership abilities may occur on the playground where a student has organized a soccer game complete with assigning everyone's positions and monitoring the rules during the game for compliance, and has placed themselves in the role of conflict-resolution referee. Another area in which you might observe outstanding leadership is within a student's peer group. More often than not, when a peer group needs to self-select a leader they will pick the person with outstanding leadership abilities whether the abilities are positive or negative. Another setting in which you might see gifted leadership abilities is when a student will intercede and translate for a teacher, a student or both during a conversation when there is limited communication due to language. Within the family context, Bernal (1978) characterizes leadership as accepting responsibilities at home that normally are reserved for older children, such as the supervision of younger siblings or helping others to do their homework. Gifted Latinx English language learners who demonstrate outstanding leadership abilities are often drawn to situations where they can be useful in their environments.

Exceptional Ability in Fine Arts

Gifted Latinx English learners do not always identify academically, but may exhibit superior abilities in any of the fine arts. The Latino culture is rich with artistry, imagination, creativity, and innovation. Latino cultural awareness and pride can be exhibited in many of the fine art genres often depicted by the use of bold colors, embedded passion and polyrhythmic rhythms. Talent observations in other areas of art may be exhibited through traditional, indigenous, and native dances, music or textiles. Consider that art is so much more than painting and sculpture. Opportunities for Latinx students to participate in the fine arts should be provided by schools and observed for potential gifted abilities.

Twice-Exceptional

While gifted Latinx learners have many strengths, some of these learners may also display twice-exceptional characteristics. The term "twice-exceptional," commonly referred to as "2e," is used to describe students with gifts and talents who also show evidence of one or more disabilities as defined by federal or state eligibility criteria (e.g., specific learning disabilities, speech and language disorders, emotional/behavioral disorders, physical disabilities, autism spectrum, etc.) (NAGC, 2020). Some common characteristics of twice-exceptional learners are:

- They have a specific or consuming interest area.
- They have a superior vocabulary.
- They show inconsistent academic performance patterns.
- They are easily frustrated.
- They have discrepant verbal and performance abilities.
- They lack organizational skills.

- They are easily distractible.
- They have advanced ideas and opinions.
- They have difficulty with social interactions (Trail, 2011).

These learners are at risk academically, socially, and emotionally because of the paradoxical view of their abilities. Twice-exceptional learners are prone to poor self-concept, reduced self-efficacy, anxiety, hypersensitivity, elevated levels of frustration, self-criticism, and poor social skills (Trail, 2011). Effective programming for twice-exceptional learners requires that educators have an understanding of giftedness as well as an understanding of their special needs. When working with twice-exceptional learners, it is important to start with a strengths-based approach to their learning and then remediate for the challenge areas as well as support for social emotional needs. When determining whether gifted Latinx learners are twice-exceptional, it is critical to recognize that learning a second language should not be an automatic referral to special education. The existence of racial/ethnic disproportionality in special education must be considered when referring Latinx learners for special education services. A team of professional educators knowledgeable in the areas of special education, gifted education, and culturally linguistically diverse learners should convene to determine whether a student is twice-exceptional.

Greene DuBois Latinx Gifted Behavior Observation Tool

Often teachers use a tally system to document the frequency of gifted behaviors observed in the classroom. The Greene DuBois Latinx Gifted Behavior Observation Tool shown in Figure 2.1 is an example of a behavioral observation tool intentionally designed for observing and documenting characteristics of gifted Latinx English language learners. This tool can also be found in Appendix C. The items on the Greene DuBois Latinx Gifted Behavior Observation Tool were designed based on the characteristics of gifted Latinx English language learners discussed in this chapter. The Greene DuBois Latinx Gifted Behavior Observation Tool is

Greene DuBois Latinx Gifted Behavior Observation Tool

When utilizing the observation tool below, remember that behavior characteristics may have positive and negative manifestations. For example, asking insightful questions may seem socially inappropriate for Latinx learners. Leadership abilities may be positive or negative.

Directions: Place a tally mark in the frequency column every time you notice the behavior characteristic when compared to the student's native peers. Write a description of the behavior in the observation notes section.

Name: _____ Date of Observation (s): _____

Examiner's Name: _____ Position: _____

Length of time the examiner has known the student: _____

Behavior Characteristics	Frequency	Observation Notes
Reads 2 or more grade levels above in heritage language		
Rapid second language acquisition		
Superior interpreter abilities *Adjusts tone, style, and register based on the interaction*		
Ability to code switch *Language and affect changes based on environmental situations*		
Easily navigates between cultures *Understands nuances and differences within cultures*		
Asks insightful questions		
Creative ability		
Advanced sense of humor *Understands idiomatic phrases, puns, and jokes in English and Spanish*		
Outstanding math potential or abilities		
Leadership abilities *Positive or negative* *Multiple settings* *With or without native peers*		
Exceptional abilities in fine arts and/or talent		

FIGURE 2.1
Greene DuBois Latinx Gifted Behavior Observation Tool

not intended to be a normed measurement tool, but rather an observation tool in which educators can note the frequency, using a tally system, of students exhibiting behaviors that align with gifted characteristics of Latinx students compared to their native peers. It is important for educators who are noting behaviors to be familiar with the characteristics of gifted Latinx learners. They should also be well acquainted with the student in order to provide an accurate observation of gifted behaviors.

There are 11 items on the Greene DuBois Latinx Gifted Behavior Observation Tool, which employs a tally system. A tally should be noted in the frequency column each time a teacher observes a student exhibiting outstanding behaviors compared with their native peers. The Greene DuBois Latinx Gifted Behavior Observation Tool, or any other observation tool that denotes gifted behaviors pertaining to Latinx English language learners, is valuable because the documented frequency can guide programming and next steps for students exhibiting a high frequency as noted in the observation tool.

When a student demonstrates high frequency on any of the items in the Greene DuBois Latinx Gifted Behavior Observation Tool or on multiple items, the next step would be to determine what type of educational intervention might need to be implemented. This could include referral for gifted identification, talent development, or providing enrichment opportunities beyond those currently being made available to the student. This tool should not be used as the sole means to identify gifted Latinx English language learners but should be included among multiple pieces of data indicating potential giftedness. The Greene DuBois Latinx Gifted Behavior Observation Tool is not normed and is merely a research-based observation tool that could suggest a student might need to be referred for further examination using other measurement tools to determine giftedness. In Chapter 3, other observation tools will be examined to support the identification of gifted Latinx English language learners.

Key Points

- The Latinx population is the fastest growing population in the United States.
- Gifted characteristics of Latinx students may display differently from those of non-Latinx students, depending on their background knowledge, access to learning opportunities, and cultural experiences.
- Some gifted Latinx learners may have high levels of verbal ability in their heritage language.
- Rapid acquisition of English is an indicator that a Latinx student might be a bilingually gifted student.
- Bilingual gifted Latinx learners are capable of high-level interpretation skills.
- Outstanding leadership abilities are frequently demonstrated by gifted Latinx learners, and can be both positive and negative in nature.

References

Castellano, J. A. (1998). *Identifying and assessing gifted and talented bilingual hispanic students* (ED423104) ERIC. https://files.eric.ed.gov/fulltext/ED423104.pdf

Castellano, J. A., & Frazier, A. D. (Eds.) (2011). *Special populations in gifted education: Understanding our most able students from diverse backgrounds.* Waco, TX: Prufrock Press.

Castellano, J., & Robertson, R. (2014). Talent development, language development and writing skills. In M. S. Matthews & J. A. Castellano (Eds.), *Talent development for English language learners: Identifying and developing potential* (pp. 15–46). Waco, TX: Prufrock Press.

Flores, A., Lopez, M. H., & Krogstad, J. M. (July 2019). U.S. Hispanic population reached new high in 2018, but growth has slowed. Retrieved September 2, 2020, from www.pewresearch.org/fact-tank/2019/07/08/u-s-hispanic-population-reached-new-high-in-2018-but-growth-has-slowed

Granada, J. (2003). Casting a wider net: Linking bilingual and gifted education. In J.A. Castellano (Ed.), *Special populations in gifted education: Working with diverse gifted learners* (pp. 1–16). Boston: Allyn & Bacon.

Hughes, C. E., Shaunessy, E. S., Brice, A. R., Ratliff, M. A., & McHatton, P. A. (2006). Code switching among bilingual and limited English proficient students: Possible indicators of giftedness. *Journal for the Education of the Gifted, 30*(1), 7–28.

Irby, B. J., & Lara-Alecio, R. (1996). Attributes of Hispanic gifted bilingual students as perceived by bilingual educators in Texas. *SABE Journal, 11*, 120–143.

Macías, R. F. (2016). Language ideologies and rhetorical structures in bilingual education policy and research: Richard Ruiz's 1984 discursive turn. *Bilingual Research Journal, 39*, 3–4, 173–199.

Marian, V., & Shook, A. (2012). The cognitive benefits of being bilingual. *Cerebrum: the Dana Forum on Brain Science, 2012*, 13. www.ncbi.nlm.nih.gov/pmc/articles/PMC3583091/.

NAGC. (2020). About NAGC. Retrieved December 21, 2020, from www.nagc.org

Olszewski-Kubilius, P., & Thomson, D. (2015). Talent development: What does it look like in practice? *Gifted Child Today, 38*(1), 5–6.

Trail, B. (2011). *Twice-exceptional gifted children: Understanding, teaching, and counseling gifted students*. Waco, TX: Prufrock Press.

U.S. Census Bureau. (2012). National Population Projections Tables. Retrieved December 21, 2020, from www.census.gov/data/tables/2012/demo/popproj/2012-summary-tables.html

Valdés, G. (2003). *Expanding definitions of giftedness: The case of young interpreters from immigrant communities*. Mahwah, NJ: Lawrence Erlbaum.

WIDA. (2014). *2012 amplification of the English language development standards Kindergarten–Grade 12*. Retrieved December 21, 2020, from https://wida.wisc.edu/sites/default/files/resource/2012-ELD-Standards.pdf

3

Culturally Responsive Assessment Practices

Using a Body of Evidence to Identify Gifted Latinx Learners

Gifted Latinx learners can be challenging to identify for a variety of reasons, including gifted identification procedures. Often, the procedures used to determine giftedness are limited and inclusive due to the type of qualifying data being collected. One of the key components of the DuBois Greene Culturally Responsive Gifted Framework is assessment (Figure 3.1), a process that involves gathering multiple and various information to create a comprehensive profile of an individual based on data (Ford, 2013).

When equitable assessment practices are integrated within a culturally responsive pedagogy, the value and importance of a student's heritage culture can be recognized. Within the context of the framework, culturally responsive assessment refers to the assessment practices being used in a gifted identification process. This does not mean to imply that tests are without bias and are culturally responsive; there are no culturally responsive tests, but there are culture-fair tests, which are equally fair to all cultural groups where there is a lack of bias in the interpretation or use of a test to classify or diagnose (Getz, 2011). It is doubtful that any test can completely eliminate cultural bias, but some tests are designed with the intention of being less biased than others.

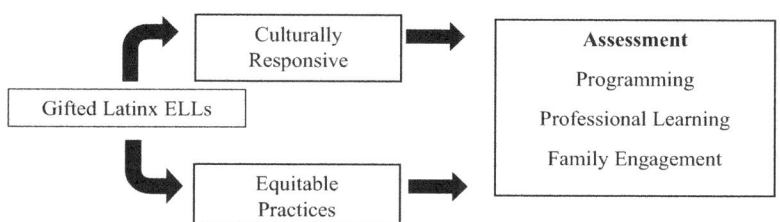

FIGURE 3.1
DuBois Greene Culturally Responsive Gifted Framework: Assessment

These generally have less of a language load, meaning that there is limited language being used in both the content and administration of the assessment tool.

This chapter provides a review of assessment tools that the authors have found to be advantageous in the identification of gifted Latinx learners. This does not mean that they are the only assessment tools that might be useful in identification of these learners, but they are the ones that the authors have found to be beneficial.

Body of Evidence

A body of evidence refers to the collection of quantitative and qualitative data gathered to create a student profile that can be analyzed for gifted traits. Quantitative measurement tools use numbers to describe and understand an individual's strengths or other characteristics (Johnson, 2004). These assessment tools can measure both ability and/or achievement. They are generally norm referenced, meaning the student's score is compared with those of other students of the same age or grade level among a population of students.

Qualitative measurement tools use words to describe and understand an individual's strengths and characteristics (Johnson, 2004). Most qualitative assessments are not norm referenced but are a measurement of feelings and actions. The most common qualitative assessment tools are behavioral observations, interviews, and student portfolios.

When identifying gifted learners, multiple pieces of data should be collected that demonstrate outstanding ability and high potential. An identification process that relies on one single score for a gifted identification limits opportunities for students who might not express gifted characteristics based on the measurement used. The use of multiple forms of criteria when developing an identification process to enhance the identification of gifted minority students has been termed "casting a wider net" by Frasier and Passow (1994). This more in-depth review of a learner can allow for greater opportunity to discover gifted traits that otherwise may not be recognized with limited traditional assessment tools. The process for gathering a body of evidence depicting the cultural identity of a gifted Latinx student is complex and may take more time than that for a student from the majority culture due to the collection of a larger body of evidence.

School districts have a choice of which assessment tools are used to collect data in the body of evidence for gifted determination. In most cases, the body of evidence (Figure 3.2) typically contains cognitive ability tests, achievement tests, and behavior observation scales.

When "casting a wider net," additional alternative tools should be considered for the expanded body of evidence (Figure 3.3 and Appendix D), such as creativity assessments,

FIGURE 3.2
Body of evidence

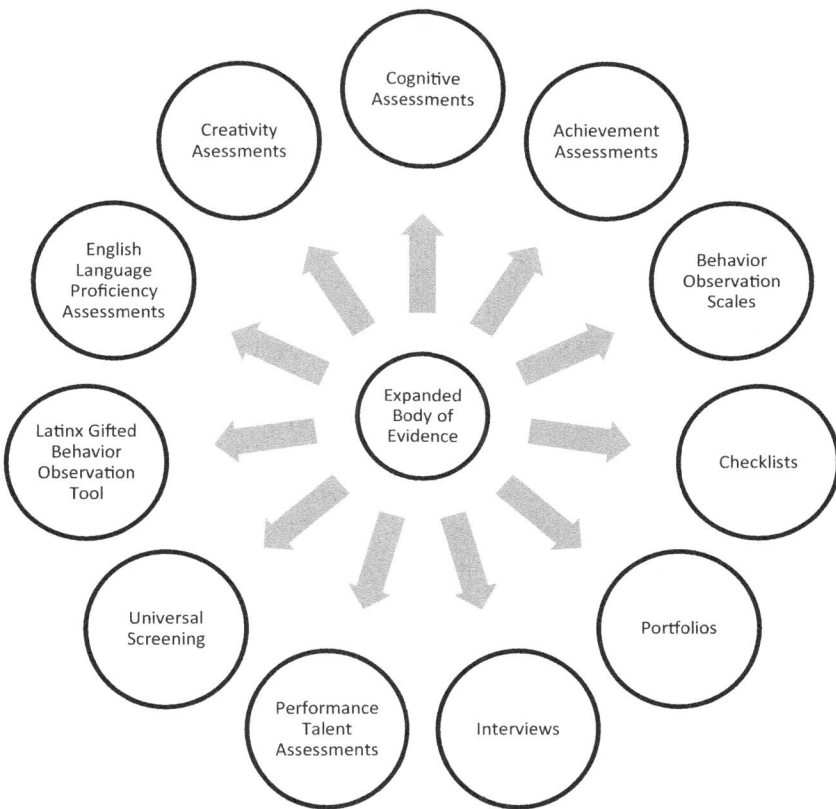

FIGURE 3.3
Expanded body of evidence

observation tools and behavior checklists that may not be norm referenced but reflect cultural experiences, language ability measurement tools, universal screening, performance talent assessments, portfolios, and interviews with both the student and the family.

When evaluating a student's body of evidence to determine gifted potentiality, it is important that a number of people evaluate the data together. An evaluation should not consist of only one person but rather a team that is knowledgeable about gifted education and English language learners. Ideally, the team would consist of a gifted education specialist, a culturally and linguistically diverse education specialist who is familiar with language acquisition, and an educator who is familiar with the student and is able to speak to the student's strengths. Also consider making a school counselor, social worker, or psychologist part of the team if needed to discuss any social emotional traits with which the student presents. The members of the team should all be familiar with the characteristics of gifted Latinx English language learners and have had specific professional learning in these areas.

Before continuing with the remainder of this chapter, the authors want to state that this portion of the book is not an endorsement for any one test or test publishing company. These are merely the assessment tools that the authors have found to be successful in their identification process for gifted Latinx English language learners. Access to different assessments varies based on multiple factors such as school district budgets, state rules and regulations around assessment, local rules and regulations regarding assessment, and additional norming. Depending on the learner's profile, the authors may use different assessments to create a body of evidence that offers multiple opportunities and modalities for the learner to demonstrate performance and potential. Remember that there is no one assessment tool that should be used as the sole means for identifying these learners. Simply stated, there should be a robust body of evidence and no one test should determine giftedness.

Cognitive Assessments

Cognitive assessments are quantitative tools that are normed on either individual administrations or group administrations of tests. These assessments measure ability (learned reasoning) and/or aptitude (a learner's intellectual potential regardless of learned skill). The authors are using the term "cognitive assessments" to refer to those ability and aptitude assessments that measure general intellectual ability (GIA), or the ability to problem solve, make connections, and manipulate abstract ideas. These assessments are not designed to measure what a student knows in a specific content area but rather are designed to predict the examinee's potential to learn and use new cognitive skills (Psychology, 2020). The following questions should be considered before administering a cognitive assessment to a Latinx student:

1. Does the student need the content to be administered in their heritage, or native, language?
2. Does the student receive extended time on assessments due to limited English skills?
3. Does the student have any accommodations due to a Section 504 Plan or Individualized Education Plan?
4. Does the student need a paper-and-pencil version of the assessment?
5. If giving an online assessment, is the student familiar with online testing and the use of technology?
6. Is the student familiar with the examiner?
7. Does the student need a scribe to assist with writing?
8. Are there practice tests, or sample questions, that the student has had the opportunity to review prior to the administration of the test? By showing students the types of questions they will receive, the examiner is giving an opportunity to review the type of question and the way questions are structured. This research-based practice is aimed at mitigating questions about how to take the assessment, not what it is asking.

Batería Woodcock-Muñoz IV

The Batería IV is designed to evaluate individuals whose native language is Spanish and is an adaptation of the Woodcock-Johnson (WJ) IV. The age range is two through 90+ and is individually administered with each subtest typically taking five to ten minutes. It is recommended that examiners have graduate-level training in educational assessment. The Batería IV has both cognitive and achievement batteries and allows for specific tests from the Batería III and WJ IV Tests of Oral Language to be added to an evaluation.

Cognitive Abilities Test (CogAT)

The CogAT measures a student's reasoning and problem-solving ability. It comprises three Batteries: Verbal, Quantitative, and Nonverbal. The age range is grades K–12 and it can be administered in a group or individually. The CogAT provides an option for further reducing language load on the Verbal Battery by using an Alternative Verbal (Alt-Verbal) scale. The Alt-Verbal scale eliminates the Sentence Completion subtest from the Verbal Battery score at levels 5/6, 7 and 8. The CogAT also offers a Nonverbal Battery. The CogAT can be administered online or using a paper-and-pencil version, and is timed at the upper grade levels. It is not recommended to use the composite score but rather the individual Battery scores when determining gifted identification for Latinx learners.

Differential Ability Scales-II (DAS-II)

The DAS-II has an Early Years Spanish Supplement Kit that measures young Spanish-speaking children's cognitive abilities. The age range is 2:6 to 6:11 years and the test is individually administered via paper-and-pencil. The subtests are translations and adaptations of the subtests from the Early Years English Battery of the DAS-II. Professionals representing Argentina, Chile, Colombia, Costa Rica, Cuba, El Salvador, Mexico, Nicaragua, Panama, Peru, Puerto Rico, Spain, and Venezuela were involved in the development of the assessment to ensure that any cultural or language issues that might affect the assessment of a child from each specific culture were addressed (Elliott, 2020).

Kaufman Brief Intelligence Tests Second Edition (KBIT2)

The KBIT2 measures verbal and nonverbal intelligence and is individually administered. The age range is from four through 90 years. There are three subtests: Verbal Knowledge and Riddles, which comprise the verbal portion, and Matrices, which embodies the nonverbal portion. The nonverbal portion of the KBIT2 can be administered as a stand-alone test without obtaining a composite score. Correct responses are accepted in Spanish. The Riddles subtest has Spanish answers provided for the examiner. The Matrices has administration instructions in Spanish. The KBIT2 is untimed and typically takes 20–30 minutes to administer; it can be administered by anyone trained in the administration of the test.

Naglieri Nonverbal Ability Test 3 (NNAT3)

Naglieri Nonverbal Ability Test Third Edition (NNAT3) is a nonverbal measure of general ability for students from Kindergarten through Grade 12. The test is available online and in a paper-and-pencil version. It can be administered to a group of students or individually. The NNAT3 is timed. The NNAT3 may be used as a universal screening tool because it is a 30-minute assessment, short in length, and has a minimized language load with analogous reasoning and problem-solving using pictures rather than words.

Wechsler Intelligence Scale for Children—Fifth Edition Spanish (WISC-V Spanish)

The WISC-V Spanish is an adaptation of the WISC-V English version. The test has an updated norming sample of children whose primary language is Spanish. The age range of the WISC-V Spanish is 6:0 to 16:11 years. The test is timed and can be administered online or in a paper-and-pencil version.

Examiners must hold a doctoral degree in psychology, education, or a closely related field to administer the test. Students can receive credit for correct responses in either Spanish or English. Parent reports are available in Spanish.

Before considering an aptitude assessment such as WISC V, DAS II, or KBIT2 with Latinx English language learners, Kogan (2001) cautions that translated assessments should be reviewed with a critical eye. Some adapted versions are translations of assessments "used in other countries that were not written with the bilingual child in mind from a linguistic nor a cultural point of view" (Kogan, 2001, p. 26). Specifically, the Latinx population in the United States has multiple Spanish dialects as well as dialectical differences within and across regions. When these differences are not considered in testing or the presentation of materials, Kogan argues that translations of assessments hold no value or purpose (Kogan, 2001).

Because of these potential cultural nuances in translated versions of an assessment, gifted education programs should ensure that all Spanish versions and culture-fair tests are normed with similar populations of students. Therefore, when researching the norming sample of a potential assessment, gifted professionals can evaluate the assessment to determine which norming groups were used, and then review their own school demographic data to determine whether the students in the sample are representative of the students within the school who will test. Each specific Latinx population (Guatemalan, El Salvadorian, Ecuadorian, etc.) with varying levels of English proficiency is not always specifically included in the norming population, thus reinforcing the need for an expanded body of evidence.

Creativity Assessments

Creativity ability tests measure creative thinking by assessing a student's fluency, elaboration, flexibility, and originality, through convergent and divergent thinking activities. The Torrance Tests of Creative Thinking (TTCT) Figural Test is timed at 10 minutes and is normed. It can be given individually or group administered. The test can be scored in house by a trained scorer or can be sent directly to the company for scoring. Individuals are also able to become officially certified to score the assessment by hand once they have received very specific training from the publisher. The directions for the Figural TTCT is available in Spanish and the titles of creative figures used in the test can be written in Spanish or English.

Achievement Assessments

Achievement tests measure what a student already knows or understands about a content area (Johnson, 2004) and does not include measurements for potential. Achievement assessments do not always demonstrate the actual knowledge a child has about information outside of school-based subjects. Children enter school with different amounts of background knowledge, which may impact the outcome of these tests for Latinx learners. Students from culturally diverse backgrounds, linguistically diverse backgrounds, and/or poverty may begin their first year of school with a 30 million-word gap (Greene, 2017; Hart and Risley, 2003). Because of this, gifted Latinx English language learners may not have the prerequisite language skills necessary to navigate English-only assessments with specific cultural references. It is therefore critical to include a robust body of evidence to support identification. Achievement tests come in various forms. The following tools are those that the authors have found to be successful in their identification process of gifted Latinx English language learners.

Aprenda: La prueba de logros en español, Tercera edición (Aprenda III)
The Aprenda is modeled after the Stanford 10 and measures Spanish-speaking students' abilities in their native language. It can be used for K–12. Reading, math, language, spelling, listening, social science, and science are the areas evaluated by the Aprenda. The reading passages in the Aprenda tests were written by published authors of Spanish children's literature in the United States, Puerto Rico, Mexico, Spain, and Central and South America (Riverside Insights, 2020). The Aprenda is untimed and can be administered as a group or individually.

Batería Woodcock-Muñoz IV
The Batería Woodcock-Muñoz IV is the Spanish version of the Woodcock-Johnson IV. As mentioned previously in this chapter, the Batería IV comprises both cognitive and achievement tests in Spanish. The achievement tests measure reading, writing, and math skills. The tests are individually administered and it is recommended that the examiner has a doctoral-level degree in psychology, education, or a related field.

Logramos, Tercera Edición (Logramos)
The Logramos is the Spanish adaptation of the Iowa Test of Basic Skills (ITBS). It measures academic progress of native Spanish speakers in the areas of reading, language, mathematics, science, and social studies. The Logramos is available online and in a paper-and-pencil version. The test uses authentic Spanish texts to allow for the content to be culturally relevant to students.

Measures of Academic Progress (MAP)

The MAP assessments measure a student's academic growth in math and reading. MAP is individually administered on a computer and has both Spanish and English assessments. The Spanish assessments are made up of items that are adapted from the English MAP version and newly created, authentic Spanish items. All the Spanish passages and items for MAP Reading Fluency are newly created, authentic Spanish content (NWEA, 2019). The MAP assessments allow for students to be assessed in both English and Spanish, which could be beneficial when assessing biliteracy or dual-language immersion students for growth in both languages.

State Achievement Assessments

Many states in the United States have end-of-year state summative assessments of students' knowledge of grade-level content-based standards. These tools sometimes offer the option for students to take these tests in Spanish at a specific grade level before having them take the test the following year in English. When reviewing state achievement scores of Latinx English language learners, educators should look for growth and *trends over time*. If a student scores at an advanced level taking the Language Arts test in their heritage language of Spanish one year and then scores proficient or even below average the next year on an English language version of the assessment, then this is a student's body of evidence that needs an additional review. The review team may want to see one more year of assessment data or, based on a larger body of evidence, this data over the course of two years may prove to be helpful. The review team, specifically an educator who understands how the student is reasoning in their heritage and their host language, will be an essential member of the committee to review data.

Test of Early Mathematics Ability-Third Edition (TEMA-3)

The TEMA-3 measures a student's math proficiency. It is untimed and is administered individually. The age range is from three years to eight years and 11 months. The TEMA-3 comprises informal and formal math concepts and skills, such as numbering skills, number-comparison facility, numeral literacy, mastery of number facts, and calculation skills (Pro-Ed, 2020). Although the TEMA-3 is not available in Spanish, the authors recommend translating instructions into Spanish and using a Spanish interpreter to administer the assessment.

English Language Proficiency Assessments

English language proficiency assessments are used to measure language development of learners whose native language is not English. One of the commonly used English language proficiency assessments is ACCESS, which stands for "Assessing Comprehension and Communication in English State-to-State for English Language Learners" (WIDA, 2014). ACCESS is administered annually to students and is available for grades K–12. The domains measured by ACCESS are speaking, listening, reading, and writing. ACCESS data can be used to demonstrate a student's rapid English language acquisition by examining growth over time. A Latinx English language learner who acquires English in half the time than is expected as measured by English language proficiency assessments is potentially a gifted English language learner due to their rapid English language acquisition.

The authors recommend that, at the beginning of each school year, educators should seek out ACCESS or any other English proficiency assessment scores across their entire district and analyze the data to determine which English language learners are progressing at a rapid rate of acquiring the English language. Educate teachers on how to examine English language proficiency data for students who demonstrate rapid language growth.

Above-Level Testing

Above-level testing, also known as off-level testing, originated with Dr. Leta Hollingworth (1886–1939) over 100 years ago (Stanley, 1990). Above-level testing is the practice of administering a test to a gifted child who is younger or in a lower grade than the group for which the test was originally designed (Warne, 2012). When using an above-level test, one can identify how much of a challenge and differentiation are needed for students. Above-level testing can also demonstrate whether a student should be subject or grade accelerated.

Observation Tools

The use of observation tools as part of a body of evidence supports the concept of "casting a wider net." Student observations in settings where outstanding potential is demonstrated can provide additional information on gifted Latinx students. Observations can be performed in a variety of ways, and the data can be qualitative or quantitative depending on the tool being used. Tools include, but are not limited to, behavior rating scales, gifted characteristic checklists, anecdotal information, and inventories. Some observation tools are normed while others are not. The following are some issues to consider before selecting someone to make an observation:

1. Observers should be knowledgeable about gifted behaviors of Latinx students.
2. Observers should be knowledgeable about gifted behaviors of English language learners.
3. Observers should compare student behaviors with their native peer group.
4. Observers should be well acquainted with the student being observed.

Observation tools can be used for individual students or for groups as a screening tool. They are subjective in nature; however, observation data can be an important part of the body of evidence. Educators who do not typically work with gifted learners should receive training on how to complete the observation tools prior to using them on a student.

HOPE Teacher Rating Scale

The Hope Scale was designed to identify high potential students from low-income families. It is a teacher rating scale for grades from Kindergarten to Grade 5, and has 11 items that measure both academic and social-emotional components. The Hope Scale has two subscales: academic and social. Although the instrument was normed during the development process, the authors of the HOPE Scale recommends against using a set cutoff score on the subscales (Gentry, Pereira, Peters, McIntosh, & Fugate, 2015). Instead, they suggest the following: use local norms with each district so that the scale truly represents the population of learners, and use the Hope Scale as part of the documentation to determine a student's potential.

Talent Observation Rating Scales
Haroutounian's (2014) Talent Observation Rating Scales measure potential talent in the areas of music, visual arts, dance/movement, and theater/drama. The Scales use art-specific criteria in the individual art areas rather than generalized gifted characteristics. Haroutounian's Scales are derived from "artistic ways of knowing," which describe the perceptual and cognitive processes inherent working through the arts (Haroutounian, 2014). These are perceptual awareness and discrimination, creative interpretation, behavior and performance, and commitment and critique.

Some school districts have developed their own scales for measuring potential talent. Many of them are aligned with criteria for talent identification in their districts. Iowa and Colorado are two states that have their own talent scales.

Kingore Observation Inventory (KOI)
The KOI serves two purposes, which makes it different from other behavior rating scales. It is a teacher observation tool used to identify gifted potential and it provides learning experiences that encourage gifted behaviors. The KOI experiences can be used as classroom activities and administered as a group, and the KOI provides exposure and opportunity for learners so they have multiple opportunities to share their strengths. The KOI has seven categories: advanced language, analytical thinking, meaning motivation, perspective, sense of humor, sensitivity, and accelerated learning. The KOI is another tool in which training is critical so that educators know how to complete the protocol for the whole class.

Greene DuBois Latinx Gifted Behavior Observation Tool
The Greene DuBois Latinx Gifted Behavior Observation Tool (Figure 2.1) mentioned in Chapter 2 was designed to identify gifted potential in Latinx learners and in Latinx English language learners. The tool is not normed and there are no cutoff scores. It was created to increase teacher awareness and engagement in discovering gifted Latinx learners and gifted Latinx English language learners, and to be used as documentation that further data should be gathered to determine a gifted identification or to help with programming needs.

Scales for Identifying Gifted Students (SIGS)
The SIGS is a nationally normed observation scale for ages five through 18. It measures seven areas: general intellectual ability, language arts, mathematics, science, social studies, creativity, and leadership. The SIGS has both a school and home scale, with the home scale provided in Spanish. The Scales are available online as well as in a paper-and-pencil version.

Performance Talent Assessments
Gifted students do not always demonstrate their giftedness academically through ability or achievement data. Some students are not gifted academically but may be gifted in other areas, such as creativity, leadership, visual arts, dance, psychomotor, drama, or music. These areas can be demonstrated through performance assessments. These can include juried performances, contests or competitions, and student portfolios.

Juried Performance
A juried performance is where students' performances are judged by content experts. Generally, students are awarded a rating or prize for their outstanding ability.

Contests
There are many opportunities for students to compete with peers in and out of school. Contests and competitions in which

students receive outstanding recognition should be added to the body of evidence as performance data.

Portfolios

A portfolio is a collection of student work over time that demonstrates outstanding ability in an academic content area or a performance area such as visual arts, music, dance, creativity, psychomotor, or leadership. The use of portfolios as qualitative information in the body of evidence for gifted identification is another pathway for students who might otherwise not be identified with traditional assessments. Portfolios allow students to display their work over a period of time, demonstrating their progress and innovation. The student products can be gathered from a variety of sources, not just at school but also at home and within the community.

A portfolio should include student reflections about each of the products. The reflections give a more in-depth look at the students' thoughts and process in creating the product. These reflections could be done through writing in the heritage language, speaking and recording their reflections (again in their heritage language), and via an informal interview between educator and student. Awards and recognitions can and should be included in a portfolio as performance data (they may support academic and talent areas). A rubric and an expert panel in the content area are essential components of the evaluation process of the student portfolio products. Haroutounian (2014) offers suggestions for rubrics and evaluation guidelines for gifted characteristics in performance areas of music, visual arts, dance/movement, and theater/drama that might be helpful for school districts in the process of developing portfolio criteria for the arts.

Building a robust portfolio will take time, and this may not be a quick gathering of data. The content will also vary based on the school setting. Students and/or educators may choose work to submit for review. When educators in particular choose work, the assignments chosen should show a learner's potential, growth, and ability in a specific area (Kogan, 2001).

Other Data

Interviews

Interviews with students, parents and community members provide qualitative information about a student's interests and strengths. They can give an alternative profile of a student that is different from a cognitive assessment, which presents only a student's academic profile. Interviews can be a supplemental tool to support information in the body of evidence when identifying for creativity, leadership, or in the performance areas.

Student interviews can provide an insight into the inner thinking of a student and where they believe their strengths may lie. They can also be used to gather information about student products and performances. Interviews can be structured or unstructured. Haroutounian (2014) has created structured student interview questions about products and performances that school districts can immediately use in their gifted identification process. The authors have provided an example of a student interview survey in English (Figure 3.4) and in Spanish (Figure 3.5) that can be used as it is, or modified for your population of students. The student interview surveys can also be found in Appendix E and the Spanish translation in Appendix F.

Parent interviews can be a critical part of the body of evidence, as they can provide additional information about a student's strengths and outside interests about which the student is passionate. These interviews can also contribute information about a student's challenges, such as testing anxiety or childhood trauma that might impact a student's educational productivity.

When interviewing parents of Latinx students, it is important to take the following suggestions into consideration. Many of these families may not feel comfortable divulging information about their child or about their family to someone they don't know or trust. It is important to build a rapport with them first before interviewing them. They also may not feel comfortable speaking with someone who is not able to communicate with them in their native language. Qualitative information gained from interviews can be a meaningful part of a student's body of evidence.

Student Interview Survey

1. What are you interested in learning about?

2. What causes you frustration?

3. What brings you joy or makes you happy?

4. Who do you trust and why?

5. Is there anything you would change about your learning experience?

6. What do you want people to know about the world?

7. What makes you "you"?

FIGURE 3.4
Student interview survey

An example of a family questionnaire created by the authors can be found in Figure 6.2 in Chapter 6 and the Spanish translation can be seen in Figure 6.3. It can also be found in Appendix G and the Spanish translation in Appendix H.

Which Test to Administer

The tools reviewed in this chapter have provided a number of options for assessing Latinx English language learners as well as observation tools that can be utilized. The question remains of where to begin. Start with student data that has already been

Encuesta de Entrevista para Estudiantes

1. ¿Qué te interesa aprender?

2. ¿Qué te causa frustración?

3. ¿Qué te trae alegría o te hace feliz?

4. ¿En quién confías y por qué?

5. ¿Hay algo que cambiaría sobre su experiencia de aprendizaje?

6. ¿Qué quieres que la gente sepa sobre el mundo?

7. ¿Qué te hace "tú"?

FIGURE 3.5
Encuesta de entrevista estudiantes

compiled at the school level, such as state testing data, English and Spanish language proficiency data, beginning and end of the year reading and math data. Give the Greene DuBois Latinx Behavior Observation Tool or another observation tool to teachers and document anecdotal teacher comments about the student. All this information can help to determine a student's area(s) of strength and guide your assessment selection. It can also minimize testing and save time. If a student's strength is math, then administer a math test rather than a reading test first. If the student is strong in their native language, then administer a test that is in their native language. Knowing a student's learning profile can help to guide the selection of appropriate assessments to be used with each student.

A student's language ability can impact test selection and can determine whether to use testing materials in English or in Spanish. It can also dictate whether a nonverbal assessment should be administered first and whether testing directions need to be translated. Another consideration when determining which test to administer is knowing a student's access and ease with technology. Some testing companies offer paper and online administration. If the student has not had a lot of experience using, or has not had frequent access to, a computer, then an online assessment would probably not be the best choice. A better test selection would be one that can be administered via paper-and-pencil. If assessments are given online, then have students practice with the technology multiple times before the day of the assessment. This will help mitigate any concerns around a student who is learning how to use the technology. The other option might be to provide the student with a technology scribe who can assist the student with the technology part of the assessment.

Other Factors

Additional factors need to be considered when selecting assessment tools to be used in a gifted identification process to identify gifted Latinx English language learners. These factors include norms, language demands, item bias, translations, and environmental influences. Administrators should be aware of these factors, and be knowledgeable about the assessment being given and accommodations that may need to be applied to the testing process.

One factor to consider is the norming population of the assessment being used. Cognitive, achievement, and some observation tools are normed, meaning that the tools are interpreted using a normative score. A normative score compares an individual's performance with the performances of other individuals who took the same test (Johnson, 2004). Typically, most tools are nationally normed, meaning that student results are compared to a national population of students who took the same assessment. It is important to know the demographics of the population to which the test was normed, to determine whether the norming sample contains representatives from the Latinx culture. The age of the instrument used should also be considered as the demographics in the United States are constantly changing, which will reflect in the demographics of the norming sample being used. Norming samples older than ten years are not reflective of current demographics.

The next factor to consider is the language demand of the assessment being given. All assessments have some language demand, some more so than others—even non-verbal assessments. An instrument that requires a high English language demand is not culturally fair for students who may not be proficient in English. One way to reduce a high English language demand is to use a nonverbal assessment.

When selecting an assessment, one should consider item bias, meaning that some of the items on the test may be more biased towards one group's language and cultural background than that of another group. There may be some terminology or references within the items that are not familiar to specific groups. For example, administrators should make themselves familiar with the instrument being given so as to ensure that the items within the assessment do not portray stereotypes, are culturally appropriate, and are not culturally offensive to the student taking the test.

In order to make intelligence tests more accessible for Latinx students, many test makers have translated and adapted them into Spanish. However, it should be noted that an exact translation may not be linguistically appropriate for all Latinx students, depending on which country they are from. The dialects vary and not all English words can be translated directly into Spanish, making the translation unclear.

There are environmental influences that can affect students and how well they perform on a test, such as time of day, distractions, and familiarity with the administrator giving the test. Early in the day, when their minds and bodies are not tired, is a good time for most students to take tests. Make sure that if students need to miss a class to take a test, the class they are missing is not one of their favorites. Tests should be individually administered when possible to allow for fewer distractions.

Local Norms

Local norms and/or group norms are a way to evaluate students using a local data sample rather than a national data sample. This process is a method by which students can be compared directly with other students in their buildings or district. The reasoning behind local norms is that comparing students with others who attend a school in another state is equivalent to comparing apples to oranges. Local norms and/or group-specific norms provide an opportunity for Latinx students to be nominated for gifted programming. Peters and Gentry's (2012) research supports the use of group-specific norms either district-wide or within a school. The use of group-specific norms for identification of either gifted or for talent development programming has been shown to enhance achievement measures, which in turn produces a more proportional representation of underserved students for gifted programs. Furthermore, Peters and Gentry (2012) suggest that combining such a practice with the use of a teacher-rating instrument will locate even more students than using group-specific norms alone.

Universal Screening

Frasier and Passow's (1994) idea of "casting a wider net" in gifted identification by using multiple criteria can be applied to universal screening. This refers to the process of administering an assessment tool to an entire population of students for the purpose of identifying high potential or gifted ability. Universally screening all students within a grade level provides information from all student groups, including those that are traditionally underrepresented in gifted education. This process eliminates teacher bias and levels the playing field in the nomination of students for gifted services. Students who might not otherwise have been looked at for gifted testing are now given access to such testing.

Universal screening tools commonly used in gifted education can be either quantitative or qualitative, depending on which measurement tool a school district chooses to use. Qualitative assessments that are commonly administered are cognitive ability assessments that have less of a language load, such as a non-verbal assessment like the NNAT3, which is a series of puzzles that require students to problem-solve.

Observation checklists can also be used as a universal screener if done across entire grade levels for all students. The Kingore Observation Inventory, for example, is one tool that can be used to universally screen students who are demonstrating gifted characteristics and could then be used as part of a body of evidence or as another entry point for additional testing.

How often should a school district universally screen students and at what grade levels? Universal screening should occur annually during the early grades from Kindergarten to Grade 2 with an additional screening at middle school. The screening data provides direction for additional steps for students to be either referred for gifted identification or talent development. Universal screening should be a part of any gifted identification process.

Tips for Administering Assessments

As mentioned earlier in the chapter, the authors' use of the term "culturally responsive assessments" does not refer to the assessments themselves being culturally responsive; rather it relates to the administration and the steps that are taken to make the testing process culturally responsive. The following recommendations will allow for an assessment to be administered in a culturally responsive manner:

- ♦ Build a relationship with students before assessing them. This will encourage a safe and trusting environment for the student.
- ♦ Prior to the administration of the actual assessment, provide opportunities for students to take practice tests of the assessment. This will prepare students with background knowledge and practice tackling tasks that they will need to perform in the assessment.

- Use a paper assessment when possible. Assessments given online place students who may have had limited access to technology at an unfair disadvantage.
- When possible, assessments should be administered in a student's native language. If that is not possible, then the assessment directions should be translated for the student in their native language.
- There should be an option for students to answer test questions in their native language without penalty.
- When possible, have a bilingual administrator administer the assessments so that language does not become a barrier for students. Students do not have to be fully proficient in English to be given an assessment for gifted identification, nor do they need to be proficient in English to develop a portfolio.
- Assessments that are not timed are the best choices for students navigating between two languages. Students who are second language learners are often provided with an extended time accommodation on assessments in accordance with state policy.
- A one-on-one testing environment is recommended, as this provides a safe environment for the student.
- Students should be given the option for the administrator to scribe for them, to relieve any unnecessary stress that the student might be experiencing during the testing.

Checklist for Culturally Responsive Assessments

Below is a checklist that educators and administrators can use to ensure that they are following best practices in assessment for the identification of gifted Latinx English language learners. A complete checklist is provided in Appendix J and includes culturally responsive gifted best practices for the other components of the DuBois Greene Culturally Responsive Gifted

Framework: Programming, Professional Learning, and Family Engagement. A blank template of the checklist can be found in Appendix L for usage with other culturally and linguistically diverse learners.

- Are there multiple assessment options that are culture-fair?
- Are the assessments available in the student's native, or heritage, language?
- Does the body of evidence contain both qualitative and quantitative data?
- Are there opportunities for students to be universally screened?
- Are there performance assessment options for students to demonstrate giftedness in the arts, creativity, and leadership?
- Is there an opportunity to demonstrate outstanding performance through academic and/or talent portfolios?
- Are language proficiency data reviewed for students demonstrating gifted potential throughout the school year? When and how often are data reviewed?
- Is the option to use local norms available?
- Are group-specific norm data available to use for either gifted identification or talent development opportunities?

Key Points

- A robust body of evidence can play a key part in the identification of gifted Latinx learners.
- A body of evidence should include qualitative and quantitative data.
- The use of local norms and/or group-specific norms can increase the identification of students from underserved populations.
- Universal screening eliminates teacher bias in a gifted nomination process.

References

Elliot, C. D. (2020). *Differential ability scales-II early years Spanish supplement.* Retrieved December 21, 2020, from www.pearsonassessments.com/store/usassessments/en/Store/Professional-Assessments/Cognition-%26-Neuro/Comprehensive-Ability/Differential-Ability-Scales-II-Early-Years-Spanish-Supplement/p/100000299.html?tab=product-details

Ford, D. Y. (2013). *Recruiting and retaining culturally different students in gifted education.* Waco, TX: Prufrock Press.

Frasier, M. M. & Passow, A. H. (1994). *Toward a paradigm for identifying talent potential.* Storrs, CT: National Research Center on the Gifted and Talented.

Gentry, M., Pereira, N., Peters, S., McIntosh, J., and Fugate, C. M. (2015). *HOPE teacher rating scale.* Waco, TX: Prufrock Press.

Getz, G. E. (2011). Culture fair test. In J. S. Kreutzer, J. DeLuca, & B. Caplan (Eds.), *Encyclopedia of clinical neuropsychology.* New York: Springer. doi:10.1007/978-0-387-79948-3_1186

Greene, R. M. (2017). *Gifted culturally linguistically diverse learners: A school-based exploration.* Unpublished doctoral dissertation, University of Denver, Denver.

Haroutounian, J. (2014). *Arts Talent ID: A framework for the identification of students talented in the arts.* Unionville, NY: Royal Fireworks.

Hart, B., & Risley, T. R. (2003). The early catastrophe: The 30 million word gap by age 3. *American Educator, 27*(1), 4–9.

Johnson, S. K. (2004). *Identifying gifted students a practical guide.* Waco, TX: Prufrock Press.

Kogan, E. (2001). *Gifted bilingual students: A paradox?* New York: Peter Lang.

NWEA. (2019). Five frequently asked questions about MAP Spanish assessments. https://www.nwea.org/blog/2019/five-frequently-asked-questions-about-map-spanish-assessments/

Peters, S. J. & Gentry, M. (2012). Group-specific norms and teacher rating scales: Implications for underrepresentation. *Journal of Advanced Academics, 23*(2), 125–144.

Pro-Ed. (2020). *TEMA-3: Test of Early Mathematics Ability* (3rd ed.). Retrieved December 21, 2020, from www.proedinc.com/Products/10880/tema3-test-of-early-mathematics-abilitythird-edition.aspx

Psychology. (2020). *Achievement, aptitude, and ability tests.* Retrieved December 21, 2020, from http://psychology.iresearchnet.com/counseling-psychology/career-assessment/achievement-aptitude-and-ability-tests

Riverside Insights. (2020). *Aprenda: La prueba de logros en Español.* Retrieved December 21, 2020, from www.pearsonassessments.com/store/usassessments/en/Store/Professional-Assessments/Academic-Learning/Brief/Aprenda%3A-La-Prueba-de-Logros-en-Espa%C3%B1ol-%7C-Tercera-edici%C3%B3n/p/100000585.html?tab=product-details

Stanley, J. C. (1990). Leta Hollingworth's contributions to above-level testing of the gifted. *Roeper Review, 12*(3), 166–171.

Warne, R. T. (2012). History and development of above-level testing of the gifted. *Roeper Review, 34,* 183–193.

WIDA. (2014). *2012 amplification of the English language development standards Kindergarten–Grade 12.* Retrieved December 21, 2020, from https://wida.wisc.edu/resources/2012-amplification-wida-english-language-development-standards

4

Culturally Responsive Gifted Classrooms: Providing Access and Opportunity

Overview

Educators often view students through their own cultural lens, which has been shaped by personal life experiences. For white, English-speaking teachers in particular, there is a privilege that comes with being a member of the dominant culture that may block an educator's ability to recognize the distinct cultural backgrounds students are bringing into the classroom. This is not a fault or criticism. Instead, it is a commentary on historical practices that continue to exist within education, which negatively impact not only Latinx English language learners, but any learner who is not part of the dominant culture. It is the responsibility of educators and administrators to ensure that culturally responsive teaching and programming are taking place. Culturally responsive programming is one of the key components of the DuBois Greene Culturally Responsive Gifted Framework (Figure 4.1), recognizing the importance of incorporating a student's heritage culture into all aspects of their learning. This includes both academic and social emotional programming.

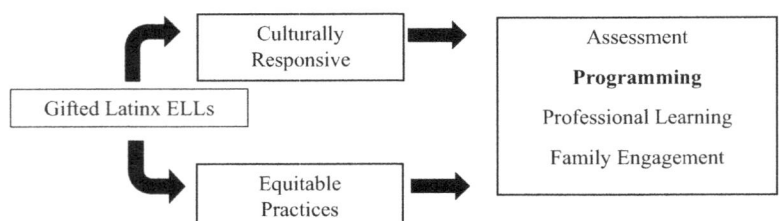

FIGURE 4.1
DuBois Greene Culturally Responsive Gifted Framework: Programming

Culturally Responsive Pedagogy

Culturally responsive education, born from multicultural education, took root during an educational paradigm shift in which there was a growing concern about the racial inequities observed and experienced in education (Gay, 2018). Culturally responsive pedagogy has its ideological beginnings in the early 1970s with multicultural education. Abrahams and Troike (1972, p. 5) suggest that in order for a racial minority students to be taught effectively, teachers must examine where cultural differences occur and "capitalize upon them as a resource." By seeing cultural differences as a value in the classroom, the teacher helps to build the dignity of the learners (1972, p. 6).

Throughout the 1970s and into the mid-1990s, multiple researchers continued to focus on the impact and importance of bicultural and diverse perspectives in the racially diverse classroom. They noted the positive impact that the act of acknowledging students' ethnic differences had on affective and academic outcomes for culturally and linguistically diverse learners. Researchers also expanded their studies to include the ways in which culture, language, literacy, and ethnicity converge in the classroom and in teaching practices in relation to the specific needs of Indigenous Americans, Latinx, African Americans, Asian Americans and Pacific Islander students (Paris, 2012). By 1995, researchers had developed multiple resource pedagogies in which creative curricular innovations and interventions were essential to support historically marginalized learners.

In 1995, Gloria Ladson-Billings published the article, 'Toward a Theory of Culturally Relevant Pedagogy (CRP)' (Ladson-Billings, 1995), in which she shared a framework for affirming students through education; this framework continues to inform current thinking and instructional practices, and has continued to be source of inspiration for other researchers (Gay, 2012, 2018; Greene, 2017; Paris, 2012) regarding culturally responsive and culturally sustaining pedagogy. Ladson-Billings shared the specific practices that educators who participated in her study used to help support their students. The authors have shared some of those practices below, as well as providing concrete examples later in the chapter for what this looks like in the gifted classroom.

Throughout all the studies and multiple theories offered, culturally linguistically diverse learners had higher achievement outcomes when the learners saw characters in literacy or the experience of others that aligned with their frame of reference—that is, their culture and language. For the purposes of this work, the authors will use Geneva Gay's term "culturally responsive pedagogy" as well as the term "culturally responsive teaching" (Ladson-Billings, 1995) because they represent the compilation of multiple years of scholarship and research. Culturally responsive teaching teaches to and through the strengths of its students and recognizes that culture is one of many strengths.

Culturally Responsive Teaching

In 1995, Gloria Ladson Billings coined the term "culturally responsive teaching" and described it as a pedagogy that recognizes the importance of including students' cultural references in all aspects of learning (Ladson Billings, 1995). Ladson Billings saw that culturally responsive teachers communicate high expectations to their learners, and that their inclusion of learning within the context of the student's culture, student-centered instruction, and culturally mediated instruction allows students to reshape the curriculum with their cultural lens. The teacher became a facilitator of instruction, encouraging culturally and linguistically diverse learners to explore their environment and engage in learning in a way that felt natural to them (Hammond, 2014; Ladson Billings, 1995; Ladson Billings 2009).

The authors view culturally responsive teaching as an act borne from culturally responsive pedagogy and subscribe to the belief that Gay (2018, pp. 36–45) shared regarding the eight specific traits, or distinguishing qualities, that create a culturally responsive teaching environment. According to Gay's (2018) compilations of research, culturally responsive teaching is:

- *validating and affirming* because it "acknowledges the legitimacy of the cultural heritages of different ethnic groups, not as legacies that affect students' dispositions, attitudes, and approaches to learning as worthy content" (p. 37)
- *comprehensive*, taking a whole-child approach that involves multiple stakeholders and formal policies
- *multidimensional*, in that it is inclusive of curriculum, as well as the climate and culture of the classroom, student–teacher relationships, and performance assessments (p. 39)
- *empowering and enfranchising* because an infrastructure is created to build student confidence by encouraging them to take academic risks and experience success
- *transformative* because it actively develops social consciousness and critical thinking—the tools needed to face oppression in any form
- *emancipatory*, both emotionally and intellectually, because it deconstructs the dominant culture schema and provides students from historically marginalized populations with the opportunity to learn about different cultures and see themselves in the curriculum
- *humanistic* because it develops the idea of human interdependence and is concerned with matters of human welfare
- *normative and ethical* in application and practice because it gives the parallel story to the Eurocentric curriculum to which students have been exposed.

Culturally Responsive Programming

Culturally responsive programming is an intentional amalgamation of representative curriculum, materials, symbols, pedagogy, and culturally responsive teaching to create programming that functions as *mirrors* and *windows* (Style, 1996). Culturally responsive programming acts as a mirror because, when done with fidelity, it is a reflection of the learners' cultural strengths and history that help them build their identity. At the same time, it can act as a window because it offers students a view into someone else's experience/perspective.

Culturally responsive programming is focused specifically on lesson planning, learning standards, curricular materials, building self-efficacy, and developing pride in culture. This can be implemented in different ways. In practice, culturally responsive programming is evidenced by the clear and obvious positive representation of student and family faces, voices, languages, and cultural symbols. This representation, known as "symbolling" (Gay, 2018), is a visual symbol of the learners' culture in the classroom and in the school. Symbolling may be observed by seeing a welcome sign on the classroom door written in the multiple languages of the classroom, including the educators' linguistic culture. Symbolling may also be incorporated through positive representative ethnic imagery that is authentic and pluralistic. This can come in the form of photographs that depict people working and learning together, or books that have ethnically and linguistically diverse characters and authors. By positively showing and acknowledging ethnicity, educators can help to build cultural identity (Gay, 2018, p. 50) and validate learners.

Another key feature of culturally responsive programming is the role that culture actively plays in the classroom. Culture is not only acknowledged, planned for, and valued; it is part of daily discourse and the educator is the facilitator of cultural competence. In this environment, educators create opportunities where learners actively engage with one another (and the educator) in critical conversations around race and culture, as well as the convergence with and divergence from the dominant culture. Educators who understand the dynamics of the culture within their classroom, and who actively orchestrate cultural constructs of inclusion and pluralism that are within the frames of their learners, are actively creating culturally responsive programming.

Culturally Responsive Gifted Education and Programming

Several key components create the foundation for culturally responsive gifted programming for gifted Latinx English language learners. Latinx learners must have true culturally responsive and sustaining gifted pedagogical practices in place, as visualized in Greene's Culturally Responsive Gifted Model (Greene, 2017) for gifted culturally linguistically diverse learners. Figure 4.2 demonstrates the marriage of multicultural gifted competencies as outlined by Ford and Trotman (2001) and Gay's (2010, 2018) culturally responsive teaching. In this model, there are culturally responsive practices there were mentioned previously, such as cultural brokering, authentic learning experiences, and high expectations. Greene's Culturally Responsive Gifted Model is also a critical piece of the DuBois Greene Culturally Responsive Gifted Framework because it helps create a structure for educators to use when planning programming.

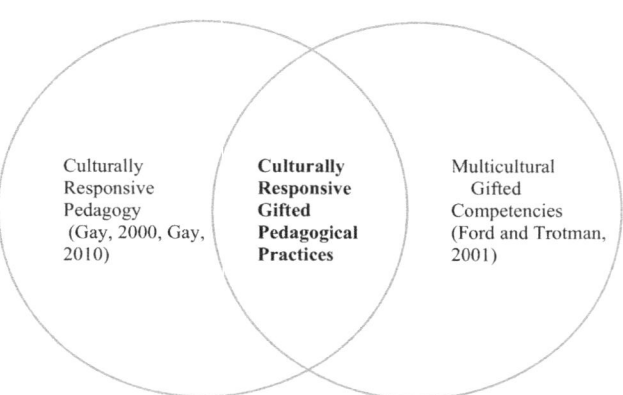

FIGURE 4.2
Greene's Culturally Responsive Gifted Model

Although Greene's Culturally Responsive Gifted Model and the DuBois Greene Culturally Responsive Gifted Framework encompass multiple diverse groups of learners, there are specific elements that are necessary in order for gifted Latinx English language learners to thrive and be seen. These pieces include honoring and maintaining the heritage language; culturally responsive gifted instructional practices and programming; social emotional learning; and enrichment opportunities. Culturally responsive gifted programming and classrooms are created when educators and administrators combine culturally responsive education with best practice in gifted education.

Honoring and Maintaining Heritage Language

Author Norma Gonzàlez (2006) states that, "Language is at the heart, literally, and metaphorically, of who we are, how we present ourselves, and how others see us." In her statement, Gonzàlez shares what educators of English language learners must understand as a universal truth for their Latinx learners: language is a critical component of the development of a student's culture and identity. Educators who internalize this understanding will be better able to actively honor and maintain Latinx English language learners' heritage, or native, language.

The integration of a student's heritage language while infusing culturally responsive content has been shown to increase student achievement and have a positive social emotional impact (Matthews & López, 2019). Heritage language should be used in student-facing curricular materials, authentic assessment, feedback conversations, instruction, and interpersonal connections as a conduit to acquiring English. Once English is acquired, the student's native language must not be dismissed or silenced.

Gifted second language learners often code switch, verbally and subconsciously, and connect abstract ideas across languages. To deny a learner's linguistic roots continued growth and maturation devalues the learner, their culture, family, and community. Instead, this asset-based approach values the deep cultural linguistic roots of the learner and is key to developing identity. The teacher is making the statement that the student's heritage language is valued and sacred.

Students must receive an education that is commensurate with their learning abilities. When access to gifted programming is not available in Spanish-speaking classrooms, gifted English language learners are denied and/or delayed in their ability to grow. Regardless of proficiency in English, second language Latinx learners must have access to advanced programming in all stages of English acquisition. The mastery of the English language should not limit Latinx learners' access to advanced programming; although, it often does.

What are the measures of success for our gifted second language learners? For gifted Latinx English language learners, success is found when students feel as if their language is valued. The validation of language occurs when gifted Latinx English language learners are able, encouraged, and enfranchised to use both their heritage language and their host language (English) throughout the day, with their peer group and with educators to engage in learning. Success can be observed when gifted English language learners are engaging in real-world problem-solving and critical thinking in both their heritage and their host languages without Spanish being sacrificed. It is seen when students are encouraged to use their heritage language long after they have become proficient in English as a means to demonstrate their understanding of a concept or even when accessing content that is new and challenging. By planning for the use of heritage language, we unequivocally demonstrate to our students and families that who they are has value.

Culturally Responsive Gifted Instructional and Programming Components

Culturally responsive gifted instructional practices are the methods of teaching that are asset and strength based, including recognizing the value of the students' language, culture and life experiences while incorporating gifted teaching strategies. These instructional practices are good for all learners, regardless of their neurodiversity; however, they are critical for gifted learners to reach their potential. This means that gifted Latinx English language learners must have access to deep and complex materials and high-impact instructional moves.

Advanced Linguistic Supports

Too often in schools, as students acquire proficiency in English, the scaffolds they are given to build their skills act as barriers to advanced content. One such scaffold, the sentence stem, helps English language learners express their thinking and acts as a structural guide for language construction. While this instructional aid is an appropriate practice to help students express their thinking, more often than not the students work with simplistic language and sentence structures; in many programs, the point is to learn how to speak and write English and both content rigor are kept at a very procedural level.

The authors, however, have seen excitement and engagement from their gifted Latinx English language learners when they have used sentence stems with complex sentence structures, advanced vocabulary, figurative language with idiomatic expressions, symbolism, and imagery. By doing this, learners are exposed to advanced linguistic structures and concepts. They receive positive messages about their ability and the value of the host and the heritage languages; thus, making this a gifted culturally responsive instructional practice. Now, as with any instructional practice that is used, it is imperative that the educator review the materials and concepts that are being presented to the learners to ensure there is no cultural mismatch with the curriculum and materials, or implicit bias that impedes student comprehension.

Developing Critical and Creative Thinking

Gifted culturally responsive instructional practices must include problem- and concept-based critical and creative thinking teaching models across all content and subjects. In actively engaging gifted Latinx English language learners through critical and creative thinking, educators will meet best practices in gifted education as well as culturally responsive education (Gay 2018) because it exhibits one of the key qualities of culturally responsive pedagogy—transformation to dismantle oppression.

To think critically is to think at a deeper level of understanding in order to form a judgment. To think creatively is to think divergently, and all learners should engage in both critical and creative thinking This practice utilizes multiple types of questions at the analysis, evaluation, and creation levels of Bloom's Taxonomy (Bloom, 1956) as well as the strategic thinking and extended thinking level questions found in Webb's (2002) Depth of Knowledge.

Critical thinking would not be complete without the use of Hilda Taba's Inductive Model or Concept Development Model, which utilizes inductive and deductive reasoning (Department of Defense Education Activity, 2006). The Concept Development Model actively engages students in macro and micro level thinking. Students think at a large conceptual level, move to the more granular level, then generalize back to a broader level. In this model, students experience expansion and construction among their thoughts. In the Concept Development Model, the educator facilitates thinking and students are active participants who determine concepts they want to study (e.g. beauty, change, power, interdependence, etc.) by asking questions. Students then personalize and give examples from their own experience to begin to construct the meaning of a concept. The students continue their deepened understanding of a concept by developing generalizations and generalized statements, or "truths," based on their concept. Next, students develop categorization systems and test their generalizations by applying the generalizations across disciplines.

Critical thinking questions may have multiple complex answers and increase the cognitive demand of a lesson or task. These critical thinking questions should be culturally responsive and constructed in a manner that is sensitive to the learner, and represent the learner's culture; the concepts involved must be those in which the learner is interested. Ideally, students will be able to create questions as they develop more agency within this type of thinking. Critical thinking questions should be used throughout all levels of English proficiency. While this instructional practice is not a new concept, studies continue to show that educators get into the trap of asking lower-level questions at a higher rate than they do critical thinking questions.

It is also imperative to remember that critical thinking questions will become culturally responsive when the questions are asking students to think about something that is happening in their community or a problem that they can help solve, and are reflective of the student's culture. If educators of gifted Latinx English language learners do not purposefully plan to incorporate culturally responsive materials and engaging learners in their preferred learning modality as often as possible, these students will continue to be left behind. When educators teach gifted culturally linguistically diverse learners to think deeply, and to think for themselves, they challenge them to critique, analyze, interpret, explain, reflect and extend (to help meet the ideals of transformation. Developing critical and creative thinking, however, also requires teaching models that support gifted learners.

Grouping and Pacing

A key component of authentic programming is ensuring that student grouping is inclusive, flexible, and fluid. The grouping of students for academic and social emotional success can be done in various forms to meet the needs of learners. Gifted Latinx English language learners, however, must be grouped with intellectual and native peers with similar strengths, as well as with an educator who is trained in gifted best practices and understands how to teach the skills necessary to become proficient in English. One such model, the schoolwide cluster grouping model (Winebrenner & Brulles, 2008), is a research-based model that has increased student achievement. In this model, students are grouped based on ability and/or achievement data, and grouped to narrow bands of differentiation for learners and teachers. When using this model with identified gifted English language learners, it is imperative to group them with other students of similar ability and/or achievement, and to have scaffolds in place for language acquisition. The schoolwide cluster grouping model can be used in bilingual classrooms, and has been used in classrooms in which the Spanish language is the dominant language. The model works across linguistic settings.

Another key instructional practice that may be overlooked with gifted English language learners is the pacing of lessons and new concepts. If a gifted English language learner who is receiving instruction in their heritage language has learned new content or makes connections within one to six repetitions, then the next concept or standard of learning should be introduced, or the educator can choose to go deeper within the standard. If the gifted English language learner is receiving instruction in the host language, the need to adjust pacing remains the same around content and standards; however, scaffolds must be in place for acquiring language so that students are able to access new content.

Acceleration

The practice of acceleration is a research-based intervention that increases academic achievement and improves social emotional outcomes. Acceleration offers students the opportunity to "match the level and complexity of the curriculum with the readiness and motivation of the student" (Colangelo, Assouline, & Gross, 2004). It is an appropriate instructional practice that should be offered to all gifted Latinx learners who move through content and curriculum at a faster pace than their peers.

Acceleration comes in different forms, and includes curriculum compacting, telescoping, single-subject, whole-grade, and radical acceleration (multiple grade levels) options (Colangelo et al., 2004). Whole-grade and radical acceleration are the most intense forms of acceleration and are typically used with highly gifted, profoundly gifted, and exceptionally gifted learners. This is not a whole-class instructional practice; instead, it is for those students whose body of evidence demonstrates mastery of standards, content, ability, and achievement data. The gifted Latinx English language learner must have access to acceleration just like their monolingual English peers. In order to accelerate in a culturally responsive manner, there must be language scaffolds in place.

It is also important to remember that acceleration into a grade level or into an advanced subject should be accessible at any grade level, provided there is a robust body of evidence. For example, pre-Kindergarten (or early childhood education) Latinx English language learners should have the opportunity to be placed in a Kindergarten accelerated classroom and still receive language support. Likewise, if a learner is in Kindergarten and has demonstrated mastery of the Kindergarten state standards in Spanish, this learner deserves to have their body of evidence and data reviewed to determine whether a move into first grade is appropriate, or if only specific subject acceleration is necessary. Again, acceleration should not be dependent on language acquisition or proficiency. When students are accelerated into the next grade level or moved ahead multiple grade levels, it is critical for the receiving educator have training in asynchronous development so that they are not taken aback or frustrated if there is a social emotional mismatch to the demonstrated intellect and ability of the gifted Latinx English language learner.

If the school is having trouble deciding whether or not a gifted Latinx English language learner should accelerate, then the authors support the use of a tool such as the research-based Iowa Acceleration Scale (IAS) (Assouline, Colangelo, Lupowski-Shoplik, Lipscomb, & Forstadt, 2020) to develop a comprehensive profile of the learner being considered for acceleration. The authors use the IAS in their practice to help make data-driven research based acceleration decisions. However, there is no one particular tool that must be used to determine the need for acceleration. No tool is perfect, and no tools to date take into consideration language acquisition rate as being a sign of cognitive ability, nor do they purposely exclude language learners. Therefore, regardless of the learner's age and language proficiency and/or rapidity of English acquisition, linguistic proficiency should not be included in the final decision to accelerate. Should a learner accelerate into the next grade level, and if they are not proficient in English, then the gifted Latinx English language learner must have scaffolded language support in place to access new learning.

Curriculum Considerations

In order for curricular materials and lesson planning to be culturally responsive, the curriculum must be of a high quality and include the experiences and perspectives of historically marginalized populations of learners. Students must see themselves represented in typical history books. Again, the curriculum can act as a window or a mirror to a students' past and identity. It is critical that Latinx learners understand more of the role of Latinx people and immigrants in the development of America. It is imperative that Latinx learners see the way the indigenous people of Latin America molded the United States.

A culturally responsive curriculum will also include matters of social justice that are important to the Latinx community. This curriculum or curricula will have high interest topics and reflect the values of the Latinx community. It will include books written by Latinx authors and have stories with Latinx characters in them. It will be mindful of dominant culture values and expressions used. Currently there is no one curriculum that meets these requirements; therefore, educators must look for these pieces within either the existing curriculum, or they must supplement. Once again, it is imperative that the curricular materials used act as both a window and mirror for all of the students in the classroom.

While there is no single curriculum that is the perfect fit for all gifted Latinx English language learners, there is a curricular model that expands upon Hilda Taba's previously mentioned work that is based on brain research related to pattern-seeking and constructivism, and that crosses cultures: concept-based curriculum. In a concept-based curricular framework, learners must grapple with abstract transdisciplinary concepts such as systems, power, change, cycles, design, order, and force, and micro-concepts that are more abstract and content-specific, such as angles, culture, tone, register, and cells (Erickson & Lanning, 2014). Erickson and Lanning (2014, p. 33) describe concepts as ideas that "transfer through time, across cultures, and across situations. They are mental constructs that frame a set of examples with common attributes." With transdisciplinary concepts that cross cultures, gifted Latinx English language learners have an opportunity to explore concepts that are universal and culturally responsive, such as justice, or language, or culture. The opportunities to have gifted Latinx English language learners construct meaning are numerous, and support best practices in gifted education and culturally responsive education by encouraging critical thinking, involving depth and complexity, and moving learners from abstract to concrete learning by making connections to self and community.

Talent Development

Talent development programming is one way to offer access and opportunity to gifted Latinx English language learners who may not yet have been identified. This programming is inclusive and is on a continuum of services that a school district could offer to support the potential of students. Talent development is a broad programming descriptor in which students receive access to advanced and complex material in an area of relative strength. Talent development students may receive programming and access in their general education classroom, within a pull-out small-group intervention, or within a push-in small-group intervention.

Talent development programming can include activities, interventions, and groupings that focus on student strengths in traditional academics, and/or the fine arts and talent domains. It can also include social emotional learning. For talent development to yield success, this type of programming should occur early, and students who receive talent development programming should be monitored for progress towards identification. In a talent development programming model, educators cultivate the potential of all learners before formal identification exists. When reviewing a student's body of evidence, an educator may not have enough data to formally identify; however, this should not limit the ability of students to access talent development programming.

Advanced Programming

Advanced and rigorous programming such as Advanced Placement (AP) courses, International Baccalaureate (IB) programs, honors classes, upper level core content, and concurrent enrollment (also known as dual enrollment with high school and college classes) are rigorous coursework and programming options that are designed to help prepare students for post-secondary life. Essentially, in AP classes, the learner takes college-level courses in high school. In IB courses, the learner is a part of a larger program that is holistic and geared towards integrated curriculum approaches. IB courses in high school can be preceded by programs in elementary and middle school, all with the same goals of preparing students for a global society and a post-secondary education or career.

Other rigorous classes such as honors and advanced classes such as Algebra II, Calculus, Chemistry and so on are often used to provide programming to gifted learners because they move at a faster pace and offer more complex curriculum quickly. Concurrent enrollment classes, or dual enrollment classes, offer a learner the ability to take a college class during the day, or outside of school, in addition to taking their high school classes. At times, the concurrent enrollment class can supplant the high school class and the learner may receive both high school and college credit at the same time. Unlike other forms of rigorous coursework mentioned, concurrent enrollment classes are classes with other college students taught by a college professor and are typically located at the college campus or undertaken via distance learning.

These programs yield success and help learners access college and the course load that comes with college. However, there are large groups of learners who are missing from these classrooms: African American, Latinx, English language learners, and other culturally and linguistically diverse groups (U.S. Department of Civil Rights, 2014). Throughout the country, studies continue to show that African American and Latinx English language learners, as well as Latinx learners, are either unable to access the programs or choose not to access them, if they exist in their high schools. Consequently, excellence and achievement gaps continue to grow (Plucker & Peters, 2020) as white English-speaking peers consist of the majority student population engaging in that type of programming (U.S. Department of Civil Rights, 2014).

There are multiple reasons why excellence, achievement, and opportunity gaps continue to grow and access is denied.

One reason, poverty, impacts the ability to access these rigorous courses significantly because there is a correlation between poverty and academic achievement, and Hispanic students are disproportionately represented in poverty compared with their white peers (Olszewski-Kubilius & Corwith, 2018). In 2009, The National College Board conducted research showing that gaps between low socioeconomic status and high socioeconomic status directly correlated with the quality of academic instruction and access to rigorous courses (Olszewski-Kubilius & Corwith, 2018, p. 39). Although poverty is not the sole reason for limited access, it is a large factor as schools may not offer AP, IB, Honors, and concurrent enrollment in low-income areas, rural areas, or low-income schools.

AP, IB, honors, and concurrent enrollment classes may not exist in school districts, as these programs may require additional funds and may not be considered part of a continuum of services. A report from the U.S. Department of Education Office of Civil Rights (2014) notes that, "A quarter of high schools with the highest percentage of Black & Latino students do not offer Algebra II; a third do not offer chemistry." If 25% of the nation's high schools do not even offer specific higher math and science courses that have been connected with college and career success, then how can gifted Latinx English language learners even begin to catch up with the other 75% of the country?

Additionally, some school districts where advanced programming options do exist in high school do not have appropriate elementary or middle school options that prepare the learner for the rigor of the advanced class. Even within districts, the more affluent schools may have pre-AP classes and Middle Year IB programs, and are able to prepare learners for secondary and post-secondary coursework. However, impoverished schools in the same district may not have those classes available. The authors have experienced this in the multiple school districts where they have worked or consulted. Without consistent access to rigorous programming beginning in elementary school or middle school at the latest, even if AP, IB, Honors, or concurrent enrollment is offered in the high school, the learner may not be able to truly access it.

This is especially true of English language learners who may be at various language acquisition stages. The previously mentioned report went on to state that English language learners "represent 5% of high school students, 2% of the students enrolled in at least one AP course, and 1% of the students receiving a qualifying score of 3 or above on an AP exam" (U.S. Department of Education Office of Civil Rights, 2014, p. 1). The data since 2009 show that more and more high schools are offering options like AP for All and IB for all, Honors for All, and opening concurrent enrollment to more learners. This is a good start, and it must be reiterated that gifted Latinx learners will need to have exposure and access to these types of classes, including the structure and rigor of these classes, beginning in elementary and middle school. These classes in high school and earlier should still offer advanced linguistic supports and the critical and creative thinking needed to prepare them for success. The lack of classes is an example of the ways in which systemic racism impacts the K–12 system.

Enrichment Opportunities
Enrichment opportunities for gifted Latinx learners should be varied and vast in nature. Enrichment in gifted education has multiple variations that include, but are not limited to, academic, programming, service delivery, curriculum, skills development, academic competitions, and systems and models (Gubbins, 2014). These enrichment opportunities serve multiple functions and can be utilized both during and outside of the school day.

Additionally, enrichment opportunities can have multiple functions. They can serve to support students both socially emotionally and academically. Enrichment activities can act as a conduit for a student's passions and interests, and may provide one of a few places where students feel they can thrive (Gubbins, 2014). They also vary in nature, quality, and purpose. Therefore, the authors support the active involvement in culturally responsive enrichment activities in which students are able to see, celebrate, support, and advocate for aspects of their culture. Many of these opportunities may come in the form of a club or group that operates within the larger community, or takes place outside of the school (i.e. at a place of worship or local community center).

In order to be equitable, culturally responsive gifted enrichment opportunities must also be offered during the school day to ensure that engaging in activities is not dependent on external needs or schedule demands that take place outside of the school day. A sound research-based, whole-school enrichment model is one way for all learners to be given an opportunity to develop a talent or interest that may or may not be academic in nature. The Schoolwide Enrichment Model (SEM), developed by Renzulli and Reis (1997) has been shown to increase student engagement and interest in gifted culturally linguistically diverse learners. In SEM, schools have the unique opportunity to collaborate and co-construct classes that are based on the staff member's or community member's talent or area of interest. This model allows students to engage with their teachers and school staff members in a non-traditional manner. The model also allows students choice about what classes they want to take or engage in. Enrichment classes can vary in nature, and can include things like crochet, a teacher's interest in mariachi music, break dancing, website building, robotics, script writing, and specific cultural interests such as ballet folklórico and textile arts.

SEM should not be language dependent, and gifted Latinx English language learners who are non-English proficient or limited-English proficient must have access to this type of enrichment. There should therefore be plans to help students to access English language if the SEM teacher is a monolingual English speaker, or alternatively the school can provide interpreters to support learners. The SEM teacher will also need training in language supports, if they have not had them before. In SEM, gifted Latinx English language learners should be able to speak and communicate in their heritage language. If the school or school community is unable to bring community members into the building, or there is an expressed interest to have a class that the community cannot offer, then the authors suggest using technology, if available, to provide distance learning for enrichment. The most successful SEM in operation is inclusive of every staff member, no matter what their role might be, and involves local community leaders and family members who have a unique skill or interest they want to share. Utilizing SEM to represent the learners, the values of the learners' culture, the language of the learners, and including the community, helps to bring multiple stakeholders together to develop a true school community where multiple groups of people are invested emotionally in the success of the learners.

Quality culturally responsive enrichment for gifted Latinx English language learners must incorporate the specific strengths and interests of Latinx learners. It should include, but not be limited to, leadership opportunities within the Latinx community, and critical and creative problem-solving (i.e. Destination Imagination, or Future Problem Solvers of America), and should embrace student gender identity (Gay Student Alliance), as well as providing clubs that honor language and culture. If bringing these types of enrichment opportunities to learners is difficult, consider the use of technology and distance learning enrichment opportunities (many are free). If utilizing the internet for enrichment is not a viable option (this may prove difficult in rural areas and/or areas of high poverty), then the authors recommend working with local community members and even neighboring communities to create access for learners.

Social Emotional Learning
Social emotional learning (SEL) is described as "the process through which children and adults understand and manage emotions, set and achieve positive goals, feel and show empathy, establish and maintain positive relationships and make responsible decisions" (CASEL, 2020). The core competencies within SEL are self-awareness, self-management, responsible decision-making, relationship skills, and social awareness (CASEL, 2020). When structured learning and competencies are enmeshed with culturally responsive gifted practices that take into consideration the sociocultural factors faced by gifted Latinx English language learners, the learners have a greater opportunity for positive outcomes.

Bibliotherapy
Educators can implement culturally responsive SEL (CRSEL) in a variety of ways throughout their instruction and programming. One way CRSEL can be facilitated is through the use of bibliotherapy with mirror and window books. The term "mirror and

window books" was first coined by Rudine Sims Bishop (1990), and refers to the concept that books can act as mirrors and reflect representations of ourselves, and they can also act as windows into the lives of other people. Latinx learners must have access to advanced reading materials in which Latinx characters or elements of their culture are represented. This is very important for students, as the majority of books that are written still focus predominantly on white characters and white Eurocentric cultures. Therefore, it is the teacher's responsibility to gather books with Latinx protagonists and preferably by Latinx authors. These books should show authentic Latinx characters whose stories are not limited to tragedies and struggles, but purposefully include success and positive characterization, and celebrate the excellence of the Latinx community.

Mentors and Mentorships

A mentor is someone who invests time, knowledge, and advice to positively impact the lives of their mentees through a formalized relationship: mentorship. In gifted education, mentorships have the ability to transform lives by nurturing the passions of all identified learners. However, in gifted education mentorships are particularly critical for helping learners with career decision-making, social and emotional support, and talent areas that look beyond academics. For under-identified populations such as gifted Latinx English language learners, mentorships have proven to be pivotal in multiple stages of the learners' development (Callahan & Dickson, 2014; Reis, Hebert, Diaz, Maxfield, & Ratley, 1995; Tomlinson, Callahan, & Lelli, 1997). It is equally important to ensure that Latinx mentors are paired with gifted Latinx English language learners (if their interests are aligned) so the learners are able to see a model of success and have a cultural connection to the mentor.

Educators can create the conditions for culturally responsive gifted classrooms by recognizing learners for the cultural and linguistic strengths they and their families bring to the classroom. By intentionally structuring academic and affective programming to include the cultural values of the learners and their families, additional linguistic support, and representation within curriculum and enrichment, educators will send the message that these learners matter and that gifted education is the proverbial floor, not the ceiling.

Checklist for Culturally Responsive Gifted Classrooms

Below is a checklist that educators and administrators can use to ensure they are following best practices in creating culturally responsive gifted programming for gifted Latinx English language learners:

- Does your school district have a strategic plan for developing culturally responsive gifted professionals?
- Are there professional learning opportunities for educators and administrators to explore and reflect upon their own cultural identity, including the role of microaggression and implicit bias?
- How do educators and administrators actively learn about the values and cultures of their school and classroom community?
- Are there gifted education professional learning opportunities for educators and administrators?

Key Points

- The mastery of the English language should not limit gifted Latinx learners' access to advanced programming, although it often does.
- Culturally responsive gifted classrooms are possible.
- Recognizing a student's culture as a strength helps to create the conditions for learners to engage and feel valued.

References

Abrahams, R. D., & Troike R. C. (Eds.). (1972). *Language and cultural diversity in American education.* Englewood Cliffs, NJ: Prentice Hall.

Assouline, S., Colangelo, N., Lupowski-Shoplik, A., Lipscomb, J., & Forstadt, L. (2020). *Iowa Acceleration Scale (IAS): A guide for whole-grade acceleration K–8*, 3rd ed. Goshen, KY: Gifted Unlimited.

Bishop, R. S. (1990). Windows and mirrors: Children's books and parallel cultures. In *California State University reading conference: 14th annual conference proceedings* (pp. 3–12). Washington, D.C.: Distributed by ERIC Clearinghouse. https://eric.ed.gov/?id=ED337744.

Bloom, B. S. (1956). *Taxonomy of educational objectives. Vol. 1: Cognitive domain*. New York: McKay.

Callahan, C. M., & Dickson, R. K. (2014). Mentors & mentorships. Critical issues and practices in gifted education, In C. M. Callahan & J. A. Plucker (Eds.),*Critical issues and practices in gifted education* (pp. 413–426). Waco, TX: Prufrock Press.

CASEL. (2020). About us. Retrieved September 13, 2020, from https://casel.org

Colangelo, N., Assouline, S., & Gross, M. U. M. (2004). *A nation deceived: How schools hold back America's brightest students*, Vol. 1. Iowa City, IO: Connie Belin & Jacqueline N. Blank International Center for Gifted Education and Talent Development, University of Iowa.

Department of Defense Education Activity. (2006). Teaching Models for Differentiation 2.5. Retrieved December 21, 2020, from https://www.dodea.edu/Curriculum/giftedEduc/upload/models_differentiation.pdf

Erickson. H. L., & Lanning, L. A. (2014). *Transitioning to concept-based curriculum and instruction: How to bring content and process together*. Thousand Oaks, CA: Corwin Press.

Ford, D., & Trotman, M. F. (2001). Teachers of gifted students: Suggested multicultural characteristics and competencies. *Roeper Review*, 23(4), 235–239.

Gay, G. (2010). *Culturally responsive teaching*. New York: Teachers College Press.

Gay, G. (2018). *Culturally responsive teaching: Theory, research, and practice*. New York: Teachers College Press.

González, N. (2006). *I am my language: Discourses of women and children in the borderlands*. Tucson, AZ: University of Arizona Press.

Greene, R. M. (2017). *Gifted culturally linguistically diverse learners: A school-based exploration*. Unpublished doctoral dissertation, University of Denver, Denver.

Gubbins, E. J. (2014). Enrichment. In J. A. Plucker, & C. M. Callahan (Eds.), *Critical issues in gifted education* (2nd ed., pp. 221–234). Waco, TX: Prufrock Press.

Hammond, Z. (2014). *Culturally responsive teaching and the brain: Promoting authentic engagement and rigor among culturally and linguistically diverse students*. Thousand Oaks, CA: Corwin Press.

Ladson Billings, G. (1995). Toward a theory of culturally relevant pedagogy. *American Educational Research Journal, 32*(3), 465–491.

Ladson Billings, G. (2009). *The dreamkeepers: Successful teachers of African American children*. New York: John Wiley & Sons.

Matthews, J. S., & López, F. (2019). Speaking their language: The role of cultural content integration and heritage language for academic achievement among Latino children. *Contemporary Educational Psychology, 57*, 72–86.

Olszewski-Kubilius, P., & Corwith, S. (2018). Poverty, academic achievement, and giftedness: A literature review. *Gifted Child Quarterly, 62*(1), 37–55.

Paris, D. (2012). Culturally sustaining pedagogy: A needed change in stance, terminology, and practice. *Educational Researcher, 41*(3), 93–97.

Plucker, J. A., & Peters, S. J. (2020). *Excellence gaps in education: Expanding opportunities for talented students*. Cambridge, MA: Harvard Education Press.

Reis, S. M., Hebert, T. P., Diaz, E. I., Maxfield, L. R., & Ratley, M. E. (1995). *Case studies of talented students who achieve and underachieve in an urban high school*. Storrs, CT: National Research Center on the Gifted and Talented.

Renzulli, J. S., & Reis, S. M. (1997). *The Schoolwide Enrichment Model: A how-to-guide for educational excellence* (2nd ed.). Waco, TX: Prufrock Press.

Sims Bishop, R. (1990). Mirrors, windows, and sliding glass doors. *Perspectives, 1*(3), ix–xi.

Style, E. (1996). Curriculum as window and mirror. *Social Science Record, 33*(2), 21–28.

Tomlinson, C. A., Callahan, C. M., & Lelli, K. M. (1997). *Challenging expectations: Case studies of high-potential, culturally diverse young children*. Retrieved December 21, 2020, from https://doi.org/10.1177/001698629704100202

U.S. Department of Civil Rights. (2014). *Civil rights data collection data snapshot: School*. Retrieved December 21, 2020, from https://ocrdata.ed.gov/Downloads/CRDC-School-Discipline-Snapshot.pdf.

Webb, N. L. (2002, March). Depth-of-knowledge levels for four content areas. *Language Arts*, *28*. Retrieved December 21, 2020, from http://ossucurr.pbworks.com/w/file/fetch/49691156/Norm%20web%20dok%20by%20subject%20area.pdf

Winebrenner, S., & Brulles, D. (2008). *The cluster grouping handbook: How to challenge gifted students and improve achievement for all*. Minneapolis, MN: Free Spirit.

5

Cultivating Culturally Responsive Gifted Professionals

Overview

In the last chapter, the authors discussed the necessary components of a culturally responsive classroom that provides access and opportunity for advanced programming to gifted Latinx English language learners. However, there is an additional influential factor that was not discussed, and it is just as important as having culturally responsive instructional practices and programming: the cultivation of culturally responsive gifted professionals through professional learning. The DuBois Greene Culturally Responsive Gifted Framework (Figure 5.1) reminds educators and administrators to examine professional learning and its role in bringing equity and access to gifted Latinx English language learners.

In order for culturally responsive gifted classrooms to exist and thrive, there must be culturally responsive gifted professionals in the room creating the conditions for inclusion and representation. Culturally responsive gifted professionals are educators and administrators who have made the commitment to understand, value, and incorporate their students' cultural preferences for learning. They value the various expressions of knowledge and unique cultural experiences of the students and families in

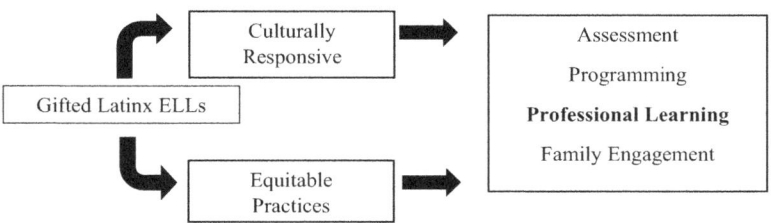

FIGURE 5.1
DuBois Greene Culturally Responsive Gifted Framework: Professional Learning

their school community. Becoming a culturally responsive gifted professional is a journey that administrators must be willing to embark on, and it cannot occur without a strategic plan focused on equity and a commitment to continual culturally responsive gifted professional learning.

Developing a Strategic Plan

When cultivating gifted culturally responsive gifted professionals, it is imperative to develop a strategic professional learning plan grounded in equity, focused on dismantling both internal and external systems of oppression. The first step begins with the commitment to develop culturally responsive gifted professionals who are able to see and understand the impact of biases on their lives and the lives of their students. It is imperative that they step outside and beyond their own cultural lens and build a cultural awareness regarding those around them.

In order to become culturally competent educators and administrators who can help gifted Latinx English language learners thrive, administrators must develop a strategic professional learning plan that will create the conditions necessary for culturally responsive gifted classrooms to exist. Figure 5.2 highlights the essential professional learning areas that must be incorporated into the strategic plan to develop culturally responsive gifted professionals.

Once a strategic plan grounded in equity is developed and educators begin to dismantle their own implicit bias, educators

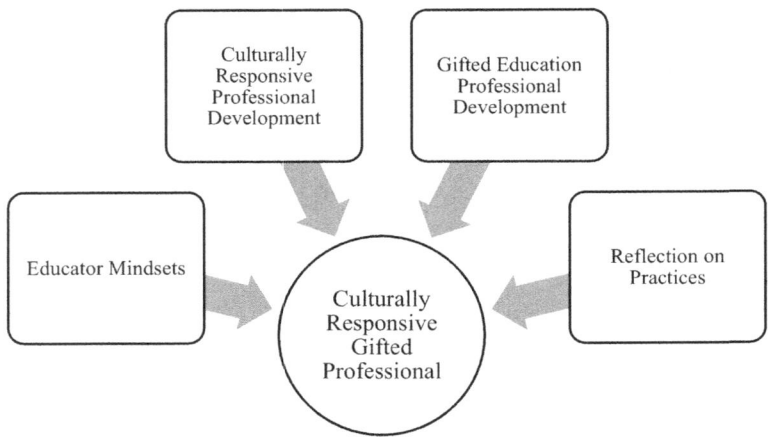

FIGURE 5.2
Strategic Plan for Developing Culturally Responsive Gifted Professionals

and administrators should utilize continued professional learning to break down the systems of oppression and build a culturally responsive gifted skill-set alongside a culturally responsive mindset. Continued professional learning should intentionally include training on culturally responsive education practices, gifted education, and culturally and linguistically diverse learners, with specific attention paid to instructional practices for English language learners and ongoing reflection.

Educator Mindsets

One of the qualities of a culturally responsive gifted professional is the ability to examine their own mindset about English language learners and the impact that has on students' educational and emotional success. A mindset is a set of beliefs, assumptions, and expectations that "we have for ourselves and others that guide our teaching practices and our interactions with students, parents, and colleagues" (Brooks & Goldstein, 2008). In education, the educator's beliefs and assumptions regarding the capabilities of their students have a significant impact on student happiness, success, and self-perception. Understanding the impact of one's mindset is imperative for the successful development of culturally linguistically diverse gifted learners, and is a key trait of a culturally responsive gifted professional. When an educator has a mindset that is fixed, deficit-based, and focused on a series of constructs that never change about their gifted Latinx English language learners, this creates a dangerous narrative for the learner because it impacts the access an educator gives, and can therefore impact the student's own self efficacy (Brooks & Goldstein, 2008; Fisher, Frey, & Hattie, 2016; Greene, 2017).

Implicit bias exists when people have an unconscious attribution of stereotypes or characteristics towards a group of people that may contradict conscious beliefs. Implicit bias is just that: implicit. It is an unconscious and unintended thought that may be positive or negative. These biases are shaped by experiences with family, friends, and the larger society. An implicit bias is something that may not be able to be identified, but it impacts interactions and reactions with the world.

Educators must ask themselves what implicit biases they have regarding the children with whom they work. When an educator sees a student excelling well in math, do they make positive attributions based on gender or race? On the first day of school, when two students walk into the classroom and one has on new shoes and clothes and the other is wearing clothing that is soiled, what unconscious judgments may have occurred about the value, worth, or backgrounds of the students? Even if the teacher consciously says and firmly believes that all students should be treated equally without judgment, an unconscious judgment might have occurred that causes the teacher to treat the students slightly differently. Upon seeing a Latinx learner, does the educator assume that the child will struggle with English, or that the child only speaks Spanish? Do they think that the student and their family are undocumented? If and when those questions come into the mind of the educator, again this may not be with negative intent or malintent. With implicit bias comes an unintended oppression of others because it continues to keep people in "boxes" and reinforces specific narratives. This evolutionary and protective trait helps humans, as a species, to make sense of the world. To challenge implicit bias is to cause cognitive dissonance and feelings of discomfort. Educators must lean into the discomfort, acknowledge the feeling, and ask themselves why the thought occurred. For gifted Latinx English language learners to be given access to programming and gifted services, implicit bias must actively be examined and disrupted.

Microaggressions are "brief, everyday exchanges that send denigrating messages to certain individuals because of their group membership" (Sue, 2010). Microaggressions are born from implicit bias and are "the constant and continuing everyday reality of slights, invalidations, insults, and indignities visited upon marginalized groups by well-intentioned, moral, and decent family members, friends, coworkers, teachers, clerks, health care professionals ... and educators" (Sue, 2010, p. xv). Microaggressions act as tiny paper cuts for historically marginalized populations (Latinx, African American, second language learners, women, etc.) and are a form of modern racism (Sue, 2010; Sue, Capodilupo, Torino, Bucceri, Holder, Nadal, & Esquilin, 2007). It is imperative for educators to not only recognize microaggressions when they see, say, or think them, but to acknowledge the impact they have on our students, families, and fellow educators.

An example of a microaggression in the classroom may occur when you ask a Latinx learner what language they speak or where they are from. By asking this question, the teacher is sending the unintended message that the student is not "from here" and is an "other" (Sue, 2010). Yet the reality could be that the Latinx learner is a third-generation American citizen who speaks only English. While the teacher did not intend to make the Latinx learner feel as if they did not belong, the teacher will have to deal with the impact of their statements. The student may or may not consciously recognize the statement as a microaggression, but repeated statements impact their social/emotional wellbeing and it is a microaggression nonetheless. With the understanding that a microaggression is a harmful consequence of implicit bias, educators must actively identify and name their own microaggressions as well the microaggressions of others. By doing this, educators will continue to create the conditions for culturally responsive gifted classroom environments.

The mindsets, implicit bias, and microaggressions that educators and administrators unintentionally carry with them lead to deficit thinking and misperceptions of the ability of culturally linguistically diverse gifted learners. In turn, these perceptions of learners lead to inequalities and inconsistencies in teacher nominations and referrals to gifted programming and also lead to underrepresentation in programming (Greene, 2017; Olszewski-Kubilius & Clarenbach, 2012). This underrepresentation in programming perpetuates and reinforces the biases around gifted programming – particularly in relation to who has a right to it and what giftedness looks like.

The mindset and perceptions of educators and administrators can perpetuate this reality as they create and implement state and local guidelines related to identification, assessment, and programming for gifted learners, which then act as barriers to access for culturally linguistically diverse gifted students. Gifted Latinx English language learners, and other groups of culturally linguistically diverse gifted learners, get caught up in the cycle of systemic racism; however, the cycle *can* and *must* be disrupted methodically and strategically so all of these learners are able to be seen and celebrated.

One way to disrupt and interrupt implicit bias is for the educator to engage in active introspection and reflection on thought patterns and behaviors. A culturally responsive gifted educator working with gifted Latinx English language learners, for example, continually asks themselves the following:

- How do I view my English language learners who are Latinx?
    - What are my perceptions of these learners and their families' capability?
    - Do I have bias?
    - Do I see having a heritage Spanish language as an asset?
    - Is having a heritage Spanish language a hindrance to being a successful learner?
- How does my cultural identity impact how I teach and how I interact with students, families, and other educators who do not look, sound, or present like I do?

- How is the way I interact with students impacting their interactions with me?
- How are the materials and activities inclusive of the learners in my classroom and how do they honor the culture of all students?
- What are my implicit biases and microaggressions?
- How do I acknowledge the impact of my words and actions while reckoning with the impact I am having on students and families?

These questions are essential to developing an internal litmus test and are the foundation for the asset-based mindsets critical to student success. These questions should be asked of every educator and with all students from historically marginalized populations.

Culturally Responsive Education

As educators actively grapple with personal mindsets and perceptions, they must also develop and refine their understanding of culturally responsive education and its potential as an equalizing force in education. In culturally responsive education, learning has "intellectual, academic, personal, social, ethical, and political dimensions, all of which are developed in concert with one another" (Gay, 2018). Furthermore, culturally responsive teachers have "unequivocal faith in the human dignity and intellectual capabilities of their students" (Gay, 2018). They seek out the strengths in students and see the value in the students' culture. This asset-based lens impacts the educator's mindset, and it is key to the development of a nurturing classroom environment, which can play a key role in the student's success.

As discussed in Chapter 4, in culturally responsive education, educators are able to see student culture as strengths, and they then adopt culturally sensitive practices such as learning about the cultures of their students, having an asset-based lens, seeing heritage language as a value, interviewing students and families to understand the values they hold, integrating relevant word problems, developing interdisciplinary units connected to each learner's interest and or community, mirror books and materials for representation, and understanding the importance of bringing in Latinx mentors.

This section of professional learning would also include training on the observable characteristics of a culturally responsive classroom for Latinx English language learners – for example, how the classroom looks visually. Attention should be paid to the realia (authentic objects from "real life" that are used to teach concepts) that represents culture and that is seen throughout instruction (whether teacher directed or student directed). Another observable characteristic, such as movement to engage with learning, may also be evident. Observable characteristics also include what the classroom sounds like (learners' engagement in real-world problems, students speaking in their heritage language or code-switching, etc.). During this portion of learning, educators would also develop their skills in facilitating the previously mentioned characteristics.

Additionally, when engaging in culturally responsive professional learning, educators would understand how to hone the skills of, and/or develop processes for, the following: setting high expectations for all learners; giving specific and authentic feedback; culturally sensitive lesson planning for the various learning preferences; and family and community engagement in the classroom. These are all critical components of a culturally responsive classroom and must be incorporated into learning for educators.

Gifted Education

Gifted learners need access to highly qualified educators who understand the learners' individual social and emotional needs as well as those who are flexible in their approach to teaching and learning. Like culturally responsive education, gifted education is not traditionally included in any preservice education experiences. Therefore, professional learning within the DuBois Greene Culturally Responsive Gifted Framework must include the very broad topic of gifted education.

This particular content would focus on the larger overview, understanding of cultural attributions and manifestations of giftedness, as well as gifted children's academic and social emotional needs. Educators would understand the difference between high-achieving learners and gifted learners within the gifted Latinx English language learner community. Educators need to have a basic understanding of the observable characteristics of gifted learners and how their giftedness manifests in the classroom, and to understand that the rate of learning is faster for gifted students and that gifted students may also have special education needs. They will see that, in a gifted classroom or among a group of gifted learners, there may be more movement and more students may be engaging and asking one another questions. They would be given tools to help them shift their thinking around the transference of knowledge in the classroom. In the gifted classroom, the educator acts as a facilitator of learning who engages their classroom through problem-solving, interest-based inquiry, complex authentic problems and tasks, and supports the metacognitive processes of learners.

Content could include the following: positive and negative manifestations of giftedness across cultures; high-impact instructional practices such as setting goals; questioning; teaching metacognitive processes; and differentiated teaching and feedback. Content could also include programming options such as cluster grouping, a concept-based curriculum, the Schoolwide Enrichment Model, exploratory models of learning such as problem- and project-based learning, critical and creative thinking, differentiation, acceleration, and pacing.

Reflection on Practices

Another key component of the strategic plan is continual reflection on the academic and affective impact of mindsets and instructional practices on gifted Latinx English language learners. A culturally responsive gifted professional is one who constantly reflects on their own practices. The culturally responsive gifted professional can review anecdotal data such as their observations of student reactions and engagement throughout the day. This is the educator who is reviewing their lesson plan for the day and thinking back through the various instructional moves, learner profiles, and how the learners engaged.

Sustainable Systems

All the work done by a school and school district to cultivate culturally responsive gifted professionals can be easily undone without the appropriate systems and structures in place to maintain and sustain culturally responsive practices and mindsets. Chapter 8 will discuss the policies and practices that are necessary for disrupting the current systems of deficit thinking and oppression. These systems and structures are imperative so that every school district and every building can start shifting the narrative for gifted culturally linguistically diverse learners.

Checklist for Culturally Responsive Gifted Professionals

Below is a checklist of questions that educators and administrators can use to ensure that they are following best practices for cultivating culturally responsive gifted professionals.

- ♦ Does your school district have a strategic plan for developing culturally responsive gifted professionals?
- ♦ Are there culturally responsive professional learning opportunities for educators and administrators?
- ♦ Are there professional learning opportunities for educators and administrators to learn about culturally and linguistically diverse learners?
- ♦ Are there gifted education professional learning opportunities for educators and administrators?

Key Points

- ♦ Culturally responsive gifted professionals are essential to the success of gifted Latinx English language learners.
- ♦ A strategic professional learning plan for culturally responsive gifted professionals should include the following content: educator mindsets, gifted education, culturally responsive education, and reflection on practice.

- Educators must actively disrupt deficit mindsets, implicit bias, and microaggressions.
- In order to teach culturally responsive gifted education, educators must understand the common principles of both aspects.
- Reflection upon practice is critical for continued growth and instructional/programmatic implementation.
- Programming must consider cultural attributions and manifestations of giftedness across cultures.
- An ongoing and sustainable system for professional learning and continued growth must be in place for professional learning to be effective.

References

Brooks, R., & Goldstein, S. (2008). The mindset of teachers capable of fostering resilience in students. *Canadian Journal of School Psychology, 23*(1), 114–126.

Fisher, D., Frey, N., & Hattie, J. (2016). *Visible learning for literacy, grades K–12: Implementing the practices that work best to accelerate student learning*. Thousand Oaks, CA: Corwin Press.

Gay, G. (2018). *Culturally responsive teaching: Theory, research, and practice*. New York: Teachers College Press.

Greene, R. M. (2017). *Gifted culturally linguistically diverse learners: A school-based exploration*. Unpublished doctoral dissertation, University of Denver, Denver.

Olszewski-Kubilius, P., & Clarenbach, J. (2012). *Unlocking emergent talent: Supporting high achievement of low-income, high-ability students*. Washington, DC: National Association for Gifted Children. Retrieved December 21, 2020, from https://files.eric.ed.gov/fulltext/ED537321.pdf

Sue, D. W. (2010). *Microaggressions in everyday life: Race, gender, and sexual orientation.* Hoboken, NJ: John Wiley & Sons.

Sue, D. W., Capodilupo, C. M., Torino, G. C., Bucceri, J. M., Holder, A., Nadal, K. L., & Esquilin, M. (2007). Racial microaggressions in everyday life: Implications for clinical practice. *American Psychologist, 62*(4), 271–286.

6

The Critical Role of the Family and Community

Defining Purpose

The authors use the inclusive term "family" to describe what traditionally has been referred to in education as "parent" engagement. What is the purpose of your family engagement? Is it for you, the educator, or the administrator to tell families about your program? Is it to learn from families about their needs while sharing information about gifted education? Is it to have families become involved in shaping the policy and practices of your program? Is it all of the above? Understanding and defining the purpose of family engagement will drive how you engage *with* and the level of engagement *from* families. Family and community engagement is so much more than holding an information night. Family engagement involves the development of a relationship of trust by district or school leaders listening to the needs of the families and asking families for their input to inform practices and policies within the gifted program. Family engagement is a key component of the DuBois Greene Culturally Responsive Gifted Framework for Latinx learners (see Figure 6.1), recognizing that families play a critical role in their students' education. Educators and administrators must be committed to work with families as partners in the educational process (Kogan, 2001).

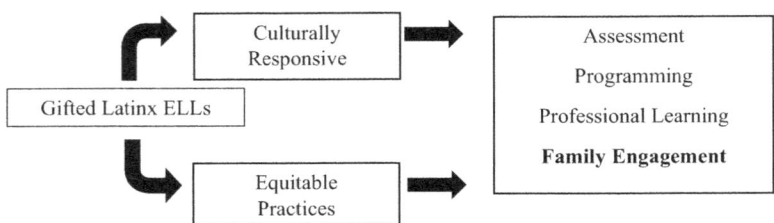

FIGURE 6.1
DuBois Greene Culturally Responsive Gifted Framework: Family Engagement

In addition to the role of family, the chapter also examines the importance of the greater Latinx community and its impact on learners.

Recruiting Gifted Latinx Learners

How do we find and recruit gifted Latinx English language learners and support their families? One way is to make information regarding gifted identification and advanced programming opportunities accessible to families in their heritage language and available in their communities. Recruiting learners may involve creative thinking, so the authors recommend involving local church organizations, Latinx community groups, local recreation centers, and other community organizations to help distribute information about gifted identification and advanced academic opportunities to Latinx families. When developing gifted procedures that address the underrepresentation of Latinx learners in gifted programs, communication with these families should be considered a vital part of the process. How, what, and when one communicates with Latinx families should be examined within any gifted program that strives to be culturally responsive.

The role of school and education within the culture of Latinx families is highly regarded, and is anchored in deep cultural belief systems. These cultural and multigenerational beliefs impact the role of educators and the role of families. As families of Latinx English language learners interact with the school, a cultural mismatch may occur when these families engage with their child's learning differently from the way an educator within the American school system may expect. In a 2007 study, Latinx parents of middle and high school students reported that their ideas of parental involvement in education included, but were not limited to, being aware of and encouraging child's abilities and career aspirations; teaching good morals and respect for others; providing general encouragement; monitoring school attendance; and providing advice on life issues (Zarate, 2007). Zarate's (2007) findings indicate that Latinx parents' perceptions of their parental involvement in education are different from those of educators. Kogan's (2001) study reinforces Latinx families' definition of parental involvement in education, which consists of constant communication of high expectations, trust in the child's educational endeavors, and enthusiasm for their child's school experiences.

Latinx family members who are not middle class or affluent, may not have the same opportunities as typical white family members to visit their children's schools for a variety of reasons, such as work schedules, transportation, and childcare demands (Castellano, 2008). While not all Latinx families are able to be physically present, educators should not interpret this as meaning the families have a lack of interest in their child's education. Often these families are working multiple jobs or do not feel safe in schools due to immigration status. Some families might feel unwelcome due to limited English skills. Others might not question the teacher's authority due to their belief that their child is in a school that is culturally responsive. Whatever the reasons are, these families are an important piece in the fabric of a school community, and should be provided with opportunities to be engaged in a school environment that is culturally responsive.

Culturally responsive gifted identification practices will provide multiple opportunities for families to be informed about the process of gifted identification. One way to communicate with families about the gifted identification process is to have an information night for Latinx families addressing Latinx gifted characteristics, the gifted identification process, and gifted programming opportunities that are available.

Another way to offer families information is to develop a family–school partnership in which there is a balance between district-focused and family-based exchanges. This includes conversations with a less formal tone that focus on culturally responsive gifted education for families, planned time for families to share their experiences and stories, problem-solving when appropriate, and transparency around district processes. No matter what is offered, it is important to make information about the gifted process and gifted programming accessible to Latinx families.

Any gathering should be held in a setting where families feel comfortable and safe, which might mean that the meeting is not held in a school building but rather in a place of worship, a local community center, or even an outdoor venue in the neighborhood. The events should be presented in the heritage language. If there is no ability to deliver the presentation in the heritage language, then interpretation should be provided. All materials, such as presentation slides, flyers, and any signage for the event, must be provided to families in the heritage language. Holding events both during the day and in the evening offers multiple opportunities for families to attend and accommodates different work schedules and family needs. Providing dinner and childcare will also be greatly appreciated by the families, and creates a caring, friendly environment. When providing food for families, be cautious of ordering food and drinks that promote cultural stereotyping. Connect with the community in which you are holding the event for donations of food and or informational pamphlets promoting local community services that can be handed out to families at the event.

Check in with families frequently to determine whether the events being offered are of value to them. Empowering and enfranchising Latinx families with tools and information about gifted procedures arms them with knowledge and promotes awareness about gifted Latinx learners within their community. Don't worry about making mistakes along the way—just start connecting with families and show that you are willing to make a commitment to them and their children.

Maintaining Family Engagement

It is critical to continue to support our Latinx families with equitable access to resources for their gifted children in order to maintain family engagement. Many Latinx families need school and community communication to be delivered in their heritage language. Communication can be distributed in a variety of ways, such as paper, email, phone calls, or person to person, and should be free of educational jargon and acronyms. Knowing which form of communication each family needs is important, as this allows them and their students to have equal access and opportunity to all information conveyed from the school.

Connecting with families of gifted Latinx learners can create a partnership between school and home for these families. One approach to connecting with families is to arrange a home visit. Home visits build positive relationships with families and convey to them that the school cares about them and their child. During home visits, when speaking with families, academic language should be replaced with a more informal register. This allows for families to be able to engage in conversation in a more relaxed and open environment in which the educator is learning about the family and is not doing the majority of the talking but rather listening. Conversation should always be in the family's heritage language; if this is not possible, then an interpreter should be provided. Listen to learn about the types of activities their students engage in outside of the school day, who they spend time with, and where they go. This helps to give a more expansive picture of the family's values and beliefs beyond a school surface level and can start to provide a deeper look into the values, norms, and expectations for the families that are not overtly stated.

If there is no opportunity for a home visit with the family, then try to engage the family in a conversation via phone. Once again, the conversation should always be in the family's heritage language and contain questions about their student's future, outside activities, and any needs of the family to gain equitable access to gifted programming. By asking questions, teachers are able to get a better sense of the whole child, family dynamics, and the important role that family and community play in the child's development of self. Educators should use the information provided to develop a strength-based profile of the whole child to create positive relationships, develop strength and interest-based programming, and identify any supports that might be needed.

When engaging a family in a home visit or through a conversation, remember the typical dominant culture interaction would ask the family to complete the questionnaire or ask each question exactly as it is written. It is not advised to read through the questions and continue to ask them one after the other. This must be a conversation, and questions should not come across as scripted. These are questions that can be embedded into any conversation and the educator should use professional judgment to accelerate trust and build relationships with the family. The authors have shared a series of questions and or talking points that can be used when engaging in a conversation with families. A sample questionnaire in English and Spanish is provided in Figures 6.2 and 6.3. The Family Questionnaires also can be found in Appendices G and H.

Families play a significant role in the recruitment of gifted Latinx learners to gifted programs and their maintenance in these programs. Reach out to Latinx families for input on what is most effective in the gifted programming at the school level and what type of enrichment activities offered are of most interest to their children. Identify key family members who are interested in becoming part of a Latinx Family Advisory Gifted Board to support outreach to families about gifted procedures and programming. Offer study groups for families focusing on information about gifted Latinx students that can provide support and a setting for them to connect with other families.

Consider building community allies within the Latinx community who support cross-cultural competence. One way to do this is by visiting local community businesses and gathering places such as the church in the neighborhood or the local market. Engage in conversations with community members about students who they identify as displaying outstanding leadership, artistic ability, and/or language abilities. Schools

Family Questionnaire

1. What are your child's strengths and interests? What has been challenging?

2. What kind of activities do you like to do together as a family?

3. What kind of activities (read, create games, play sports, etc.) does your child like to do outside of school?

4. What are your hopes and dreams for your child?

5. What kind of needs or challenges do you have that might keep your student from participating in enrichment or extension activities?

6. Are there any resources that you need at home (books, materials to support your child's interests, etc.) to support your child?

7. What other things would you like for us to know about your child?

FIGURE 6.2
Family questionnaire

have been such a place of disenfranchisement for many Latinx students and families that building cross-cultural competence among families, community members, and educators creates a school–community alliance that benefits all stakeholders.

A culturally responsive gifted program will offer learning opportunities for families in their heritage language. This could be offering Latinx families of gifted students social emotional support by inviting them to join a gifted support

Cuestionario familiar

1. ¿Cuáles son las fortalezas e intereses de su hijo? ¿Qué ha sido un desafío?

2. ¿Qué tipo de actividades les gusta hacer en familia?

3. ¿Qué tipo de actividades (leer, crear juegos, practicar deportes, etc.) le gusta hacer a su hijo fuera de la escuela?

4. ¿Cuáles son sus esperanzas y sueños para su hijo?

5. ¿Qué tipo de necesidades o desafíos tiene que podrían impedir que su estudiante participe en actividades de enriquecimiento o extensión?

6. ¿Hay algún recurso que necesite en casa (libros, materiales para apoyar los intereses de su hijo, etc.) para apoyar a su hijo?

7. ¿Qué otras cosas le gustaría que supiéramos sobre su hijo?

FIGURE 6.3
Cuestionario familiar

group for families in their heritage language led by a native Spanish speaker. The gifted support group could provide families with an opportunity in a safe environment to learn more about gifted children, to be able to express their parenting challenges, and to learn how to become an educational advocate for their child.

Checklist for Culturally Responsive Family Engagement

Below is a checklist of questions that educators and administrators can use to ensure that they are following best practices for family and community engagement in the identification of and programming for gifted Latinx English language learners.

- How is information about gifted identification and advanced programming being communicated to Latinx families?
- Are Latinx families being given multiple opportunities and ways to engage in conversations with teachers and administrators about their child? Are these conversations asset based?
- In what ways are Latinx families engaged in the school community?
- In what ways is the school inviting Latinx families in?
- How does the school recognize and incorporate the strengths of Latinx families into the classroom?
- Is there a partnership with Latinx families and teachers to promote the education of the child?

Key Points

- Communication with Latinx families in their heritage language is vital to promote equitable access to gifted programming opportunities.
- Home visits build relationships with families.
- Build cross-cultural competency among families, community members, and educators to form a school–community alliance.

References

Castellano, J. S. (2008). Critical issues and best practices in promoting equity and excellence for gifted Hispanic/Latino students. *Gifted Education Communicator, 39*(4), 24–30.

Kogan, E. (2001). *Gifted bilingual students: A paradox?* New York: Peter Lang.

Zarate, M. E. (2007). *Understanding Latino parental involvement in education: Perceptions, expectations, and recommendations.* Los Angeles, CA: Tomás Rivera Policy Institute.

7

Case Scenarios

Overview

This chapter presents authentic case scenarios depicting Latinx student profiles in both school and home environments. When reading through these case scenarios, reflect upon your own bias and stereotypical depictions of Latinx English language learners. What biases—implicit or explicit—exist? Do you stereotype Latino students and their families? Stereotyping any student population is damaging to their access to educational opportunities. Consider your own personal cultural background and the lens through which you view English language learners who are Latino. Are you culturally responsive to your students and their families? The case scenarios presented are not intended to stereotype Latinx families in any way. These are stories of families with which the authors have worked in their practice. Take a look at what changes you can make to become a culturally responsive educator and a talent scout for recognizing gifted English language learners who are Latinx. In this chapter, the authors have provided a Body of Evidence and Programming Plan in Figure 7.1 for documentation of student data and gifted programming options. The Body of Evidence and Programming Plan is also located in Appendix I.

Body of Evidence and Programming Plan

Student Name:	Date(s) of BOE review:
Age:	Language Spoken at Home:
Grade:	Referred by:
Body of Evidence	
Ability/Aptitude Data:	Achievement Data:
School Rating Scale/Observation Data:	Home Rating Scale/Observation Data:
Student Strengths:	**Student Interests:**
Gifted and Talented Programming	
Student Engagement:	Family Engagement:
Social Emotional Learning:	Enrichment Opportunities:
Community Connections:	Other:

FIGURE 7.1
Body of evidence and programming plan

Body of Evidence and Programming Plan

The remainder of this chapter will focus on presenting five case scenarios of gifted Latinx English language learners. A narrative of the student and family profiles will be given, as well as data pertaining to the student's body of evidence and gifted programming recommendations.

Case Scenarios

Student Profile A: Eliana, Six and a Half Years Old, First grade

Eliana is a first grader who is fluent in both Spanish and English. She attends a bilingual school. Eliana is often placed in a separate part of the classroom to do independent work as she completes her class assignments quickly. She has a difficult time engaging with her native age peers as they often ridicule her for being so academically advanced. During recess and lunchtime, Eliana prefers to be with an adult or often reads by herself.

Home

Eliana's parents are divorced. She spends most of her time with her mother and sees her father periodically. Eliana has a younger brother who is four years old. Prior to the divorce, the home environment was tumultuous and unsafe. Eliana's mother receives child support and works, but the family struggles financially. Both parents have limited English skills.

Nomination

Eliana was nominated by her first grade teacher, Mrs. Altimira, to go through the gifted identification process and to be considered for grade acceleration mid-way through the school year.

Body of Evidence

- Eliana was administered an ability test. She scored in the 97th percentile on the nonverbal portion of the assessment.
- Eliana was administered the end-of-year first grade (98%) and second grade (68%) district math assessments.
- Eliana was administered the Logramos reading battery. She scored in the 99th percentile.

- Eliana was administered an English reading assessment. The results indicated that she is reading at a second-grade level in English.
- Writing samples in both English and Spanish were collected and reviewed.
- Mrs. Altimira completed the Greene DuBois Latinx Gifted Behavior Observation Tool (Figure 2.1 and Appendix C) which indicated that Eliana's gifted behaviors were beyond those of her native peers.
- A normed school rating scale measuring behaviors observed in the classroom was completed by Mrs. Altimira; it indicated that general intellectual ability was in the 98th percentile, language arts in the 95th percentile and math in the 98th percentile—all strength areas for Eliana.
- A normed home rating scale in Spanish was completed by Eliana's mother, with several areas, such as leadership, language arts, and math, marked in the 95th percentile or above.

After a team of educators reviewed the body of evidence, it was determined that Eliana met the criteria for gifted and talented identification and the criteria for grade acceleration.

Programming

Based on Eliana's academic and social emotional profile, the following programming options were recommended:

- Family engagement
  - Home visit with family to help build family school relationships (Family Questionnaire Figures 6.2 and 6.3, and Appendices G and H).
  - All family communications translated.
  - Collaborate academic and affective advanced learning goal(s) with family.
  - Connect mother with other Latinx families who have gifted children.

Box 7.1 Body of Evidence and Programming Plan for Eliana

Student: Eliana	**Date(s) of BOE review**:
Age: 6.5 years old	**Language(s) spoken at home**: Spanish
Grade: 1	**Referred by**: Mrs. Altimira
Body of evidence	
Ability/aptitude data: Nonverbal Ability Test—97th percentile	**Achievement data:** End of year Grade 1 math assessment—98th percentile End of Year Grade 2 math assessment—68th percentile Logramos—99th percentile Reading Level in English Grade 2 level Writing samples in English and Spanish
School Rating Scale/Observation data: Greene DuBois Latinx Gifted Behavior Observation Tool indicated that Eliana's gifted behaviors are beyond those of her native peers Normed school rating scale—General Intellectual Ability 98th percentile, Language Arts 95th percentile, Math 98th percentile	**Home Rating Scale/Observation data:** Leadership—95th percentile Language arts—96th percentile Math—97th percentile
Strengths: Bilingual ability Reading Math	**Interests:** Reading Math
Programming	
Student engagement: Grade acceleration mid school year to Grade 2 Lunch reading group for students that enjoy reading	**Family engagement:** Home visit All family communications translated Connect mother with other Latino families who have gifted children School counselor—recommendations of grant monies available
Social emotional learning: Friendship group with native peer second graders monitored by school counselor	**Enrichment opportunities:** School librarian to support Eliana's passion for reading
Community connections: Local community food share program	**Other:**

- Meet with school counselor for recommendations of grant monies available to help support the family financially.
- Student engagement
  - Grade acceleration to Grade 2 mid-school year.
  - Lunch reading group for students who enjoy reading.
- Social emotional learning
  - Connect Eliana with a native peer group of girls to form a friendship group monitored by the school counselor.
- Enrichment opportunities
  - Connect with school librarian to support Eliana's passion for reading.
- Community connections
  - Local community food share program.

Student Profile B: Joseph, Eight Years Old, Third Grade

Joseph is a third grader who attends a public school. He was born in Mexico and moved to the United States when he was five years old. When he moved to the United States, he was able to read, write, and speak in Spanish only. Because of this, Joseph was considered Non-English Proficient (NEP) and was placed in a Kindergarten English language acquisition class, where the majority of the instruction was delivered in Spanish. His teacher, a native Spanish speaker, quickly realized that Joseph was speaking with complex sentence structures that she did not observe in her other students and was able to read chapter books in Spanish. The teacher began offering talent development opportunities and differentiated programming to Joseph so she could meet his advanced academic needs. Over a period of three years, Joseph quickly acquired English by going from Non-English Proficient (NEP) to Fluent English Proficient (FEP). He is fluent in both Spanish and English and often translates for his parents during parent–teacher conversations. Joseph is a hard worker and excels in academics. He is a leader at school and has expressed an interest in becoming the President of the United States when he grows up.

Home

At home, Joseph speaks only Spanish. His parents speak limited English, often relying on Joseph to play the role of interpreter for them in public settings such as school, the grocery store, the bank, and medical offices. Joseph often translates English documents for his family. His parents work several jobs and rely on Joseph to take care of his younger sister when they are working. Joseph's family attends church weekly and is very connected with the local Latino community.

Nomination

Joseph was nominated by his third grade homeroom teacher, Mrs. Gray, to go through the gifted identification process at his school.

Body of Evidence

- Joseph's documented three-year growth from NEP to FEP demonstrated rapid language acquisition and was noted as achievement data.
- Joseph was assessed using the Aprenda to measure his reading ability in Spanish. He scored in the 96th percentile.
- An English language proficiency test was administered to Joseph, demonstrating that he is on grade level in English.
- A Spanish language proficiency test was administered to Joseph, demonstrating that he is above grade level in Spanish.
- A portfolio of writing samples demonstrating Joseph's ability to write fluently in both Spanish and English. This data was added to Joseph's body of evidence and noted as achievement data.
- Mrs. Gray completed a normed school rating scale measuring behaviors she observed in the classroom setting. Several of the areas measured, such as language arts, leadership and motivation were 95th percentile or above, demonstrating Joseph's advanced ability in these areas compared with his native peers.

- Mrs. Gray completed the Greene DuBois Latinx Gifted Behavior Observation Tool (Figure 2.1 and Appendix C), which indicated that Joseph's gifted behavior characteristics are beyond those of his native peers.
- A normed home rating scale in Spanish was completed by Joseph's mother, with several of the areas such as leadership and motivation marked as 95th percentile or above, indicating that Joseph displays advanced ability in these areas.

After a team of educators reviewed the body of evidence, it was determined that Joseph met the criteria for gifted and talented identification.

Programming
Based on Joseph's academic and social emotional profile, the following programming options were recommended:

- Family engagement
  - Home visit with family to help build a family school relationship (Family Questionnaire (Figures 6.2 and 6.3, and Appendices G and H).
  - All family communications translated.
  - Collaborate academic and affective advanced learning goal(s) with family.
  - Social emotional family support group with other Latino families of gifted children held in the heritage language, focusing on gifted topics (held at the family's church).
- Student engagement
  - Student Interview Survey (Figures 3.2 and 3.3, and Appendices E and F) to be completed by student.
  - Research project focusing on pathways to presidency.
  - Attend Legislative Day at the state capital.
  - Other leadership opportunities in civics, including internships at the state or local government levels.

Box 7.2 Body of Evidence and Programming Plan for Joseph

Student: Joseph	**Date(s) of BOE review:**
Age: 8 years old	**Language(s) spoken at home:** Spanish
Grade: 3	**Referred by:** Mrs. Gray
Body of evidence:	
Ability data: Not applicable	**Achievement data:** NEP to FEP—three years English language proficiency test—on grade level in English. Spanish language proficiency test - above grade level in Spanish. Aprenda—96th percentile reading in Spanish
School Rating Scale/Observation data: Leadership—99th percentile Language Arts—95th percentile Motivation—98th percentile DuBois Greene Latinx Gifted Behavior Observation Tool: Multiple gifted behaviors observed	**Home Rating Scale/Observation data:** Leadership—95th percentile Motivation—97th percentile
Student strengths: Bilingual ability Reading	**Student interests:** Government Politics
Programming	
Student engagement: Student interview survey Passion project: Pathways leading to presidency Mentor Opportunities to utilize bilingual ability	**Family engagement:** Home visit All communications translated Gifted parent support group in heritage language
Social emotional learning: Bibliotherapy Peer group focusing on gifted topics with school counselor	**Enrichment opportunities:** Student Council Latino Advisory Gifted Student Board Legislative day at the capital Other leadership opportunities in civics, including internships at the state or local government
Community connections: Church Youth Group Leadership opportunities at church	**Other:** Attend summer camp for gifted kids

- Social emotional learning
  - Bibliotherapy focusing on gifted Latinx learners.
  - Adult mentor with a knowledge and passion for politics assigned to student.
  - Sessions with school counselor and gifted peers to discuss gifted topics.
- Enrichment opportunities
  - Leadership opportunities through Student Council at school.
  - Opportunity to become a member of the District Latinx Student Advisory Board.
- Community connections
  - Connect with student's church about leadership opportunities within the church community.
  - Opportunity to attend a summer camp for gifted students offered at the local university.
  - Seek out scholarship and donations from local business to help support the financial aspect of summer camp.

Student Profile C: Valeria, Ten Years Old, Fifth Grade

Valeria is in fifth grade and has a quiet, shy demeanor. She was diagnosed in third grade with dyslexia and receives services from special education. Valeria enjoys art and can be found constantly doodling and drawing in all of her classes at school, but because she is a student who receives special education services her teachers have not considered her a candidate for gifted education. Valeria recently entered a local art contest with the encouragement of Mr. Flores, her school art teacher. She placed first in her age division and second overall.

Home

Valeria's mom works as a server in a local restaurant. Paying the family's bills is challenging as her hours vary from week to week. Valeria has two younger brothers and helps her mother take care of them. Valeria's mother has limited English skills. She is enrolled in an adult English class at Valeria's school, which meets weekly. They have extended family in the community with whom Valeria spends time weekly. The family attends church services weekly.

Nomination

Valeria was nominated by Mr. Flores, her school art teacher, to go through the gifted identification process at her school.

Body of Evidence

- First place art award from local art contest.
- Valeria was administered a normed creative ability test. She scored in the 96th percentile overall for creative ability.
- Mr. Flores completed a normed school rating scale measuring behaviors he observed in the art classroom. Valeria's creativity score was in the 98th percentile, indicating that she has advanced creative abilities compared with her native peers.
- Mr. Flores also completed the Greene DuBois Latinx Gifted Behavior Observation Tool (Figure 2.1 and Appendix C), which indicated that Valeria's artistic and creative abilities were beyond those of her native peers.
- A normed home rating scale in Spanish was completed by Valeria's mother, with several of the areas such as leadership and creativity marked as 95th percentile or above.
- A portfolio of art works created by Valeria was collected to demonstrate Valeria's outstanding artistic and creative ability.

After a team of educators reviewed the body of evidence, it was determined that Valeria met the criteria for gifted and talented identification and the criteria for a twice-exceptional student.

Programming

Based on Valeria's academic and social emotional profile, the following programming options were recommended:

- Family engagement
  - Home visit with family to help build a family school relationship (Family Questionnaire (Figure 6.2 and 6.3, and Appendices G and H).

Box 7.3 Body of Evidence and Programming Plan for Valeria

Student: Valeria	**Date(s) of BOE review**:
Age: 10 years old	**Language(s) spoken at home**: Spanish
Grade: 5	**Referred by**: Mr. Flores
Body of evidence	
Ability/aptitude data: Creative ability test—96th percentile Art portfolio—outstanding performance rating	**Achievement data**: First place—local art contest Art portfolio—outstanding performance rating
School Rating Scale/ Observation data: Creativity score 98th percentile Greene DuBois Latinx Gifted Behavior Observation Tool—artistic and creative abilities beyond those of native peers	**Home Rating Scale/ Observation data**: Leadership 95th percentile Creativity 96th percentile
Student strengths: Art Creativity	**Student interests**: Art
Programming	
Student engagement: Incorporation of art into all content areas Creative ways to demonstrate knowledge in content areas Art mentor Art contests	**Family engagement**: Home visit All communication translated Twice-exceptional family support group in heritage language
Social emotional learning: Latinx artist audio books Twice-exceptional student peer group	**Enrichment opportunities**: School Art Club Opportunities to create art for school-wide events
Community connections: Connect with Valeria's church about artistic opportunities Local Latino artist to mentor Art opportunities within the local community	**Other**: Collaboration with gifted education and special education to accommodate Valeria's strengths and challenges

- All family communications translated.
- Collaborate academic and affective advanced learning goal(s) with family.
- Social emotional family support group with other Latino families of gifted children held in Spanish, focusing on gifted and twice-exceptional topics; held at the family's church.
♦ Student engagement
  - Student Interview Survey (Figure 2.2 and 2.3, and Appendices E and F) to be completed.
  - Provide art supplies for Valeria to use in her home.
  - Provide opportunities within all content areas for Valeria to be able to incorporate art into her learning.
  - Allow for creative ways for Valeria to demonstrate knowledge of content.
  - Enter art contests, both locally and nationally.
  - Meet with art teacher once a week for art mentoring and individualized instruction.
  - Gifted education and special education teams working together to accommodate Valeria's strengths and challenges.
♦ Social emotional learning
  - Audio books focusing on gifted Latinx learners and artists from heritage culture.
  - Gifted peer twice-exceptional student group working with school counselor, focusing on twice-exceptional topics.
♦ Enrichment opportunities
  - School art club.
  - Opportunities at school to create art for school-wide events (such as artwork for flyers, logos or school apparel).
♦ Community connections
  - Connect with student's church about creative and artistic opportunities within the church community.
  - Connect with a local Latino artist to mentor Valeria.
  - Art opportunities within the local community.

Student Profile D: David, 11 Years Old, Grade 6

Home
David is the youngest child in his family. His parents are farmers who sell their products to the local *mercado*. Due to the nature of their work and long hours, David's parents are not available to help David with his class assignments or homework. David's older brother and sister do, however, help him with his classwork when he needs assistance. His father is bilingual and his mother has limited English skills. The primary language in the house is Spanish. When they do have time together, David's family enjoys swimming at the local recreation center, watching movies, and attending church. David takes pride in helping his mother expand her English vocabulary by playing board games such as Monopoly and Scrabble in English with her.

School
David is a soft-spoken, kind individual who is considered by adults to be "socially well adjusted" in school; he easily navigates between different peer groups, both those for whom English is the heritage language and those for whom Spanish is the heritage language. His teachers remark that he is a joy to have in class because he follows their directions and is a hard worker. David enjoys participating in the after-school ballet folklòrico classes taught by a local dance group, which specializes in the artistry of social and ceremonial dances of indigenous people from Mexico. He is often complimented by his dance instructor for his technique and performance in class. Because he has the ability to quickly memorize choreography as well as improvise and intuit steps, the other students look to him as a leader in the class.

Nomination
As part of an established review process at David's school, the gifted coordinator and the English language specialist collect end-of-year state summative assessment data and compare data sets across years to analyze trends in achievement over time. In doing this, they search for any growth that might indicate gifted

potential for their Latinx English language learners. They also look for discrepancies in scores over time when language used in the assessments changes from Spanish to English, which occurs in fourth grade. In third grade, David demonstrated advanced performance on the state language arts assessment which was taken in Spanish. As a fourth grader, David was required to take the state language arts assessment in English and demonstrated grade-level proficiency.

Body of Evidence

- David demonstrated advanced performance on the third-grade state summative language arts assessment taken in Spanish.
- David demonstrated grade level proficiency on the fourth-grade state summative language arts assessment taken in English.
- David was administered the KBIT Matrices Battery and was in the 97th percentile.
- David's language arts teacher, Mrs. Campbell, completed the Greene DuBois Latinx Gifted Behavior Observation Tool (Figure 2.1 and Appendix C), which indicated that David's gifted behaviors were beyond those of his native peers.
- A normed school rating scale measuring behaviors observed in the classroom was completed by Mrs. Campbell, indicating that language arts (95th percentile) and creativity (95th percentile) were strength areas for David.
- A normed home rating scale in Spanish was completed by David's family, with several of the areas such as leadership, language arts and creativity marked as 95th percentile or above.
- David's dance instructor completed the music and dance/movement portions of Haroutounain's (2014) Talent Observation Rating Scales. The rating indicated a high recommendation for admission to a gifted/talented program in the areas of music and dance/movement.

After a team of educators reviewed the body of evidence, it was determined that David met the criteria for gifted and talented identification.

Programming

Based on David's academic and social emotional profile, the following programming options should be considered:

- Family engagement
  - Home visit with family to help build a family–school relationship (Family Questionnaire, Figures 6.2 and 6.3, and Appendices G and H).
  - All family communications translated.
  - Collaborate academic and affective advanced learning goal(s) with family.
  - Social emotional family support group with other Latinx families with gifted children engaged in learning more about gifted Latinx learners.
- Student engagement
  - Exposure to books that are authored by Latinx writers and written in both Spanish and English.
  - Advanced language arts class in English with scaffolding in Spanish as needed.
  - Product choice boards in which David is able to choose how he wants to demonstrate his knowledge of standards or concepts. Choices should incorporate creative thinking, dance, and leadership, and should be offered across content areas.
- Social emotional learning
  - Bibliotherapy focusing on Latinx ballet folklórico dancers and other Latinx artists.
  - Regular social emotional check-ins with a trusted adult in the building who understands the social emotional complexities David will face as he develops his cultural identity.
  - Connect David with an eighth-grade peer mentor who can help explain and ease the transition from elementary to middle school.

Box 7.4 Body of Evidence and Programming Plan for David

Student: David	**Date(s) of BOE review:**
Age: 11 years old	**Language(s) spoken at home:** Spanish
Grade: 6	**Referred by:** State testing data—demonstrating growth over time
Body of evidence	
Ability/aptitude data: KBIT Matrices Battery 97th percentile	**Achievement data:** Advanced performance—Grade 3 state summative language arts assessment taken in Spanish Proficient level—Grade 4 state summative language arts assessment taken in English
School Rating Scale/Observation data: Normed observation tool—language arts 95th percentile and creativity 95th percentile Haroutounain's Talent Observation Rating Scales indicating advanced talent abilities in music and dance/movement Greene DuBois Latinx Gifted Behavior Observation Tool—gifted behaviors were beyond those of his native peers.	**Home Rating Scale/Observation data:** Normed Observation Tool in Spanish completed by the family with several of the areas such as leadership, language arts and creativity marked as 95th percentile or above
Student strengths: Language arts, dance, creativity	**Student interests:** Dance, native culture
Gifted and talented programming	
Student engagement: Exposure to books that are authored by Latinx writers and are written in both Spanish and English. Advanced language arts class in English with scaffolding in Spanish as needed Product choice boards—choices incorporating creative thinking, dance, and leadership should be offered across content areas.	**Family engagement:** Home visit with family building relationships (Family Questionnaire) All family communications translated. Collaborate on academic and affective advanced learning goal(s) with family
Social emotional learning: Bibliotherapy focusing on Latinx ballet folklórico dancers and other Latinx artists Social emotional check-ins with a trusted adult in the building eighth-grade peer mentor	**Enrichment opportunities:** Continue ballet folklórico School talent show Offer additional dance opportunities, either in person or via remote instruction
Community connections: Work with local church leaders to sponsor David at a dance camp or to help fund dance lessons	**Other:**

- ◆ Enrichment opportunities
  - ◆ Continue ballet folklórico.
  - ◆ Opportunity to participate in school talent show.
  - ◆ Offer additional dance opportunities, either in person or via remote instruction.
- ◆ Community connections
  - ◆ Work with local church leaders to sponsor David at a dance camp or to help fund dance lessons.

Student Profile E: Alejandro, 15 Years Old, Tenth Grade

Alejandro is a tenth grader who attends a public high school. He was born in the United States to immigrant parents from Colombia and speaks both Spanish and English fluently. Alejandro excels in math but finds school boring and is often non-compliant, which has led some of his teachers to label him as a troublemaker. He has commented to his family that the content in most of his classes do not include people of color and this is a point of frustration for him. As part of Alejandro's identity development, he recently shared with his family that he identifies as a member of the LGBTQIA+ community.

Home

Alejandro's mother and father both work long hours and sometimes on weekends. His father and mother have limited English skills but are able to communicate with the school in both languages when needed and do not need Alejandro to interpret. Alejandro participates in the local community center's youth program and has shared his frustrations about school with the youth director, Mr. Pacheco, who he considers his mentor. Alejandro is often inspired by his life experience to create murals. He recently created a wall mural on the outside of the community center that showcases the idea of cultures connecting together to make the world a better place. Alejandro's family attends church each week and often volunteers at the local food bank.

Nomination

Alejandro was nominated by Mr. Pacheco to go through the gifted identification process at his school. Mr. Pacheco is a youth director at the local community center, which recently sponsored the school district's gifted and talented outreach meeting in which characteristics of gifted learners were shared with families in attendance. During the meeting, Mr. Pacheco spoke with the coordinator for the event and asked if someone at the school level could look further into a gifted art identification for Alejandro.

Body of Evidence

- A portfolio of photographs of Alejandro's wall murals was added to the body of evidence and noted as performance data.
- Alejandro was administered a nonverbal ability test. He scored in the 97th percentile on the assessment.
- Alejandro's state math assessment data from fourth to eighth grades were reviewed, demonstrating advanced math ability trending over multiple years.
- Aleljandro's algebra teacher, Mrs. Gonzales, completed the Greene DuBois Latinx Gifted Behavior Observation Tool (Figure 2.1 and Appendix C), which indicated that Alejandro's gifted behaviors were beyond those of his native peers.
- A normed school rating scale measuring behaviors observed in the classroom was completed by Mrs. Gonzales. It indicated that math (98th percentile) and creativity (95th percentile) were strength areas for Alejandro.
- A normed home rating scale in Spanish was completed by Alejandro's family, with several areas such as leadership, artistic ability, and math marked as being in the 95th percentile or above.

After a team of educators reviewed the body of evidence, it was determined that Alejandro met the criteria for gifted and talented identification.

Programming

Based on Alejandro's academic and social emotional profile, the following programming options were recommended:

- Family engagement
  - Home visit with family to help build family school relationships (Family Questionnaire, Figures 6.2 and 6.3, and Appendices G and H).
  - All family communications translated.
  - Collaborate academic and affective advanced learning goal(s) with family.
  - Social emotional family support group with other Latino parents of gifted children in heritage language, focusing on gifted topics, held at the local recreation center.
  - School counselor consultations with family members to discuss ways to support Alejandro's gender and cultural identity.
- Student engagement
  - Student Interview Survey (Figures 3.2 and 3.3, and Appendix E and F), which indicated that Alejandro felt he was not being challenged in school and was not being offered advanced coursework opportunities.
  - Advanced art course added to Alejandro's coursework at school.
  - Plan a local exhibition to display and celebrate Alejandro's wall mural art.
  - Advanced math courses added to Alejandro's coursework.
  - Alejandro will be given an opportunity to work with his teachers to review his courses for culturally relevant authentic experiences.
  - Assignment of a Latinx mentor who is an art expert.
- Social emotional learning
  - Bibliotherapy focusing on gifted Latinx people and Latinx artists.
  - Sessions with school counselor and gifted Latinx peers to discuss gifted topics and cultural identity.
- Enrichment opportunities
  - Opportunity to become a member of the District Latino Student Advisory Board.

Box 7.5 Body of Evidence and Programming Plan for Alejandro

Student: Alejandro	**Date(s) of BOE review**
Age: 15 years old	**Language(s) spoken at home:** Spanish/English
Grade: 10	**Referred by:** Mr. Pacheco
Body of evidence:	
Ability data: Portfolio of wall mural art work Nonverbal ability test—97th percentile Torrance Test of Creative Thinking—95th percentile	**Achievement data:** State math assessment data, Grades 4–8, demonstrating advanced ability trending over multiple years
School Rating Scale/Observation data: Normed school rating scale—math 98th percentile, creativity 95th percentile Greene DuBois Latinx Gifted Behavior Observation Tool: Multiple gifted behaviors observed	**Home Rating Scale/Observation data:** Normed Home Rating Scale—95th percentile
Student strengths: Art Math	**Student interests:** Art Cultural identity Community service
Programming	
Student engagement: Student interview Advanced art course Advanced math courses Art mentor Art exhibition Work with teachers to create culturally relevant course content	**Family engagement:** Home visit All communications translated Social emotional family support group to discuss gifted topics in heritage language Family consultations with school counselor to support gender and cultural identity
Social emotional learning: Bibliotherapy focusing on gifted Latinx people and Latinx artists Gifted Latinx peer group to discuss gifted topics with school counselor	**Enrichment opportunities:** District Latino Student Advisory Board School Art Club School theatre set design team School math team Engage with Gay Straight Alliance (GSA) club
Community connections: Connect with Alejandro's church about art opportunities within the church community	**Other:**

- ♦ School Art Club.
  - ♦ School theatre set designer
  - ♦ School math team.
  - ♦ Engage with Gay Straight Alliance (GSA) club.
- ♦ Community connections
  - ♦ Connect with student's church about art opportunities within the church community.

These case scenarios and programming recommendations demonstrate that each learner's profile and body of evidence form the foundation for academic and affective gifted programming. Each gifted Latinx English language learner is unique, and therefore a continuum of programming options must be offered based on their profiles. In order to sustain student and family engagement, multiple stakeholders must be invested in designing and supporting a personalized gifted culturally responsive learning experience for identified gifted Latinx English language learners. By intentionally incorporating nontraditional elements such as community involvement and family engagement, the gifted program is honoring and valuing the Latinx learners' culture and identity with multiple wraparound supports.

Implications

These case scenarios are examples of how school, family, and community working together to provide a differentiated educational experience for gifted Latinx students can be empowering for everyone involved. These scenarios are not meant to represent all Latino students, but rather to provide a snapshot of the unique students with whom the authors have worked. As case scenarios, they demonstrate the diverse and complex lives of students and families. They also highlight the need for a comprehensive body of evidence, alternative identification practices, and family engagement when programming for gifted Latinx students.

Key Points

- The body of evidence data can guide academic and affective gifted programming.
- A student's strengths and interests should be the foundation of their gifted programming.
- Gifted programming should consist of academic engagement and social learning opportunities.

Reference

Haroutounian, J. (2014). *Arts Talent ID: A framework for the identification of students talented in the arts*. Unionville, NY: Royal Fireworks.

8

Recommendations for Policy and Practice

> How do we injure the system enough so that it does not go back to the way it was?
> E. Fergus (personal communication, January 2020)

Gifted education as a field still has much to do in the area of providing equitable access to gifted programming for gifted Latinx English language learners. This is a social justice issue in which gifted education professionals must continue to challenge and question systems of inequity. Students of color deserve the right to have access to educational opportunities that are so easily given to students from the majority culture. The previous chapters have provided guidance on how to create a culturally responsive gifted program based on the components of the authors' Culturally Responsive Gifted Framework for Latinx learners depicted in Figure 8.1 and Appendix B.

The DuBois Greene Culturally Responsive Gifted Framework was designed to provide a structure to guide educational professionals on their journey to developing a comprehensive culturally responsive gifted program. In combination with the checklists found in Chapters 3, 4, 5, and 6, this framework can be used to examine a school or school district's current policies and practices to identify strengths and areas for change. The remainder of this chapter outlines the authors' recommendations, which should be considered when making transformational systemic changes to gifted practices and policy.

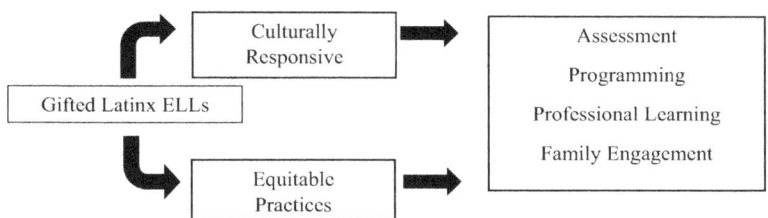

FIGURE 8.1
DuBois Greene Culturally Responsive Gifted Framework: Latinx ELLs

Recommendations for Practice

The DuBois Greene Culturally Responsive Gifted Framework can be utilized to analyze your current systems and practices guiding gifted education. In order to use the Framework in this way, the authors suggest that the reader compare each component of the Framework to their own current practices and determine what practices are in place; of those practices, what is working well; and what evidence they have to support their metrics. Success may be quantitative in the form of increased numbers of identified students, or it could be qualitative and be observed through student and teacher self-efficacy statements.

Once readers feel confident about understanding which of their processes are working well, they should shift to what needs to be improved. Even a practice that currently exists, such as universal assessment, may still need to be improved by offering exposure to the types of questions required, or ensuring that families are communicated with effectively, to support gifted Latinx English language learners, their families, and their teachers. As you are doing the program review and examining your own programming and practices, it is important to collect a body of evidence, as is done in identification. More examples and recommendations are captured in the subsequent sections.

Assessment

The first and most significant recommendation the authors have for assessment is to develop a strategic plan regarding culturally responsive gifted assessment practices. The first step in that planning is understanding how the historical oppression in gifted education continues to impact learners with linguistic diversity. The historical exclusion of second-language learners from gifted education programs is critical to remember so there is a commitment to researching and utilizing culture-fair assessments to support the identification of giftedness in Latinx English language learners. When reviewing and analyzing current practices, educators must remember that no assessment is culture-free; however, psychometricians have designed culture-fair assessments to specifically reduce bias. These assessments are considered to be culture-fair because the validity of assessment interpretation is equal and fair across cultural groups.

While there are no culture-free or even culturally responsive assessments, the practices an educator puts in place when assessing a learner can and should be culturally responsive. Indeed, it is imperative that when considering assessments and assessing the potential in gifted Latinx English language learners, the practices that educators use to identify and assess are undertaken in a culturally responsive manner so students feel socially and emotionally supported in the most conducive testing environment possible.

When utilizing the DuBois Greene Culturally Responsive Gifted Framework as a guide for reviewing assessments, district and or school level policies, and practices, educators must first develop a strategic plan for assessment of gifted Latinx English language learners. The strategic plan for assessment must include culturally responsive and equitable practices that have the following logistical consideration: deciding *when*, *where*, and *how* to assess a learner. For example, for the Latinx English language learners in the school community, it is culturally responsive and equitable in practice to review the calendar for culturally significant or important holidays that are not celebrated by the majority culture. During this calendar review, it is also critical to know any social emotional factors that may impact a learner's ability to access the assessment on that day. At face value, this simple act of reviewing the calendar and then planning accordingly may seem rather basic and considered common sense; however, the authors have made this transgression and know its negative impact on a learner. Additionally, when a non-majority culture's holidays or important celebrations are repeatedly missed or scheduled over, educators send a message about valuing culture, and implicitly state which culture is important.

Additional calendar considerations for which the authors have planned include understanding and modifying assessment windows around the schedules of students whose families are migrant workers and understanding the disruption that may be caused at home. It is important to know that the family members may not be in the primary household for months, or that the learner may also assist and help with work, because this can potentially impact both social emotional needs and academic needs. Some Latinx learners with whom the authors have taught or worked have families who travel back to their native home in Central or South America for the summer. if there is a large population of Latinx English language learners, or Latinx learners, who travel to Central or South America for periods of time, then the test administrator and the assessment planner should take that into consideration. By purposefully scheduling assessment (ability and achievement) around the learner's schedule and cultural needs, the gifted education program is able to demonstrate respect for the learner and their culture.

The plan for administering assessments must also include planning for *where* the assessment will take place. The assessment should be in a location at the school where the learner feels most comfortable. It is inappropriate to assess a learner in a space that is unfamiliar to the learner. Therefore, a culturally responsive practice for assessment will include showing an unfamiliar space to a learner before the day of the assessment. It is also imperative to establish a positive relationship with the learner as quickly as possible prior to having them assess so that, again, they are able to feel safe while being assessed. Consider what areas of the school a student may or may not feel comfortable in, based on their profile. For example, if the person assessing the student knows that the learner has had a challenging experience with a seventh grade teacher, and the test must take place in that classroom because the teacher is the only one with a free classroom, then wait to assess the learners on a different day so that as many social emotional considerations as possible can be planned for.

The strategic plan for culturally responsive assessment and assessment practices should also include *how* the learner will be assessed. Ideally, Latinx English language learners will be assessed in their heritage language. If that is not available, then the learner should have access to an interpreter. If the learner is more comfortable with low-tech options for assessment, then those should be implemented when possible (paper version vs. computer based). If there is no low-tech option available, then the learner should be exposed to the technology two to three times before taking the assessment, and they should be afforded the opportunity to practice the prerequisite technology skills required to take the assessment.

The strategic plan must also include administering a universal assessment for giftedness across one or more grade levels that is fully inclusive of students with special education needs and who are on Individualized Education Plans (IEPs) or have a Section 504 plan. The universal assessment must also be given to any student in the chosen grade level, regardless of what is considered to be positive school behavior. Furthermore, the universal assessment should be inclusive of all levels of language proficiency. Finally, there should be evidence of Latinx English language learners are part of the normed population. Ideally, the plan includes the use of local and/or group-specific norms before moving to national norms (Peters & Gentry, 2012; Peters, Rambo-Hernandez, Makel, Matthews, & Plucker, 2019). The universal assessment is administered with all the previously mentioned culturally responsive practices in place to support student social and emotional wellbeing.

As a reminder, the universal assessment is one piece of a larger and expanded body of evidence. As the expanded body of evidence is defined in the strategic plan, the body of evidence should include a balance of qualitative and quantitative data. The time required to train test administrators and teams to look at the body of evidence must also be considered.

To summarize, when reviewing current systemic practices ensure that the strategic plan for gifted Latinx English language learners includes, but is not limited to, the following:

- Develop specific guidelines for assessing Latinx English language learners for gifted programming and include language proficiency considerations.
- Logistical considerations
  - Calendar consideration for religious and secular holidays of cultural significance.
  - Time of year when assessments are given (consider all communities and their schedules).
  - Where the assessment will physically take place.
  - Scheduling considerations for breaks, and ensuring the student does not miss their favorite class or subject should they have one (whenever possible).
  - Technology proficiency and the need to build in time to expose learners to technology.
  - Build in time to meet the learner and develop a positive relationship prior to giving an assessment.
- Universal assessment practices
  - Choose an assessment that is culture-fair.
  - Must truly be universal by including students who are designated as Non-English Proficient (NEP) or Limited English Proficiency (LEP).
  - Must be inclusive of students who receive specialized supports and special education services through IEPs and/or under Section 504.
  - Focus on norm-referenced ability and achievement assessments that use Latinx English language learners as part of the normed population.
  - Utilize local norms and even consider school-based demographic norms as qualifying criteria.
  - Include non-normed referenced assessment tools such as the Greene DuBois Gifted Latinx Behavior Observation Tool.

- Choose more than one grade to universally assess at a time and vary the types of assessments used at those grade levels.
- Consider the role of performance-based assessments that help demonstrate giftedness.
- Build a comprehensive body of evidence that includes qualitative and quantitative data in the student's heritage language.
- Utilize academic and talent portfolios to demonstrate potential as well as performance.
- Choose assessments based on the learner's profile and learning preferences. This practice is best utilized when giving individualized assessments such as the Wechsler Intelligence Scale for Children V (WISC-V) or a Kaufman Brief Intelligence Test, 2nd Edition (KBIT2). Consider the language proficiency of the learner and which assessment will be most appropriate based on its strengths. The goal is to gain a deeper understanding of the learner and allow them to demonstrate their potential

Programming

Culturally responsive gifted classrooms can and do exist. They are created when educators and administrators combine culturally responsive education with best practice in gifted education. As identified in the DuBois Greene Culturally Responsive Gifted Framework, programming is a significant component of culturally responsive gifted education and serves as a reminder that district-or school level policies and practices must exist to ensure that gifted Latinx English language learners have the opportunity to access high-impact programming through culturally responsive and equitable practices.

For gifted Latinx English language learners to thrive, valuing a learner's language as well as supporting their language acquisition must also be incorporated into the culturally responsive programming and cannot be excluded from gifted education. Too often, language learners are not identified as gifted and talented, or as having a need to accelerate learning, until after they have become proficient in English. Once the learner becomes proficient in English, then statistically they have a higher chance of being identified and receiving the opportunity to engage in programming for gifted learners (Castellano, 1998). The authors have experienced two main reasons for this phenomenon: linguistic bias in assessment and the programmatic practices of both English language learner programs and gifted education programs. The authors ascribe to the talent development belief that when an educator teaches their students as if they are all gifted, then all students will benefit.

Additionally, a school district and or a school must commit to actively naming culturally responsive gifted programming as the foundation of learning for gifted Latinx English language learners. When this is identified and committed to, the school and or district will then have to allocate resources and time to ensure teachers have an understanding of best practices within culturally responsive and gifted pedagogies as well as have the ability to support English language learners as they acquire English. These are three complex pedagogies, and with the proper programming support, students will feel supported, honored, and validated for who they are.

In order to develop culturally responsive gifted programming for gifted Latinx English language learners, the authors recommend developing a strategic plan for creating culturally responsive gifted classrooms and implementation of culturally responsive gifted programming. The first part of the strategic plan for a culturally responsive classroom developed for gifted Latinx English language learners includes identifying the components necessary for gifted culturally responsive classrooms. These elements must include a proficient understanding of culturally responsive pedagogy, teaching, and programming. There must also be a proficient understanding of gifted pedagogy, instructional moves, and research-based programming so the educator is able to differentiate for their learners' needs and choose the most appropriate practices. Lastly, the classroom must use research-based best instructional practice in linguistic education and teaching language acquisition.

The first component of the plan incorporates culturally responsive gifted programming through the intentional inclusion and maintenance of the Latinx English language learners' heritage language into the classroom. Honor and maintain the gifted Latinx English language learner's heritage language by planning for the intentional integration of the student's heritage language while they are in various stages of acquiring English, including once they have reached proficiency. Typically, when an English language learner has reached proficiency, they are "exited" from their sheltered language program or bilingual program and removed from a classroom of other learners who have similar culture and values. When the student is exited from one program and placed into a mono-English classroom, they may no longer have a peer group of learners who speak the same language academically. Yes, the students may speak it casually to one another, but the language is not used to support academic conversations as it was prior to the learner becoming proficient in English. As this happens, education leaders need to start questioning the implicit value statements about language that students are receiving and internalizing.

Once gifted Latinx English language learners are proficient in the host language (English), the authors advocate an alternative educational option that includes maintaining and sustaining the learners' heritage language in their English classroom setting. Actively maintaining and sustaining the heritage language of Spanish can be done in multiple ways. For example, the educator can still offer curricular materials in Spanish and expose learners to books and other media in both Spanish and English. The educator can also encourage both casual and academic conversations in Spanish. Because gifted learners appreciate choice in directing aspects of their education, and because choice builds self-agency, it would be appropriate to offer gifted Latinx English language learners the opportunity to demonstrate their knowledge or competency in a subject in either the host or heritage language. Educators can also engage in critical feedback conversations in the heritage language, and develop an informal and interpersonal connection with students and their families.

The authors are not suggesting that educators must be fluent in Spanish; however, experience with the gifted Latinx English language learner community has shown that it is important to make a concerted effort to learn specific words, phrases, or idiomatic expressions that are dialectically representative of the learner because it shows investment. Educators who are already fluent in Spanish can still grow by understanding the dialectical differences between regions should they have a varied Latinx community in their classroom or school. By learning these phrases (or by becoming proficient in Spanish), the educator builds empathy and shares the experience of learning a language alongside their families. This additional perspective gained by the educator has the potential to positively impact relationships with students and their families.

Additional components for the strategic plan should include gifted instructional and programming strategies that are essential to the success of culturally linguistically diverse gifted learners, such as high-level critical and creative thinking. Different questioning strategies and models for critical and creative thinking were explored in Chapter 4 and can be developed in a culturally responsive manner. By including critical and creative thinking and encouraging gifted Latinx English language learners to think critically and creatively, the educator is equipping the learner with mental tools and developing mental processes so learners are able to solve complex problems. The Glossary of Education Reform (Great Schools Partnership, 2016) lists critical and creative thinking as twenty-first century skills that will help learners become future problem-solvers and independent thinkers. In this way, educators are teaching students *how* to think and not *what* to think.

The act of thinking independently to solve problems is something that research has shown to be less prevalent in culturally linguistically diverse classrooms when compared with white, English-speaking peers (Greene, 2017; Swanson, 2006). The act of excluding this type of instructional practice and programming reinforces deficit mindsets; it is a branch of implicit bias and systemic racism because it sets the proverbial bar low for all culturally linguistically diverse learners and keeps systems of oppression in place.

Additional culturally responsive gifted programming components should be considered, such as appropriate flexible and fluid grouping of learners as seen in the schoolwide cluster grouping model (Brulles & Winebrenner, 2011), which can be used as part of a larger continuum of programming for gifted learners at all levels of language acquisition. In the schoolwide cluster grouping model, students are grouped based on ability and/or achievement, and the band of differentiation is intentionally narrowed so the educator who is trained to work with gifted learners is able to help them feel success and thus to grow. The schoolwide cluster grouping model has shown positive academic outcomes for all learners, and can be used with English language learners (Brulles, Peters, & Saunders, 2012; Brulles, Saunders, & Cohn, 2010; Matthews, Ritchotte, & McBee, 2013).

Programming for gifted Latinx English language learners should also include the opportunity for acceleration, either whole-grade level, in content, or through compacting. If a student is demonstrating advanced ability and mastering standards quickly, then it is appropriate for educators to explore the role of acceleration for the learner. Like the schoolwide cluster grouping model, acceleration has been shown to be an appropriate intervention that yields positive academic success (Assouline et al., 2020). Therefore, the authors recommend that a school has a plan for the acceleration of Latinx English language learners regardless of their language proficiency. This plan must include the use of a data-driven body of evidence that demonstrates student mastery of content such as the Iowa Acceleration Scale (Assouline et al., 2020) as well as ability and social emotional considerations.

The acceleration plan should include considerations around operational concerns such as time to collect the body of evidence and communicate with families, as well as the school's master schedule and common content blocks. Common content time across grade levels is important for those students who have subject, or content, acceleration. It is also critical to have language acquisition supports available in the advanced grade for the learner to access. Ideally, if the learner is non-English proficient or limited English proficient, and shows mastery of a subject, then the learner will be able to move to the next grade level standards as they are learning English. Other operation considerations in the plan should include teacher planning time and opportunities for vertical teaming and social emotional support in the advanced grade for the learner to address any asynchronous development needs.

It has been the authors' experience that operational concerns are a large concern for school administrators because they may not have the infrastructure to make acceleration possible. Therefore, the authors suggest working with school leaders or district level administrators to work through logistical challenges to support the needs of the learners. For example, if the fifth-grade gifted Latinx English language learner is ready for sixth-grade mathematics, and sixth grade is in another physical location, then alternative solutions such as bringing the curriculum to the learner, using distance learning, or having district-provided transportation should be considered. The authors challenge the idea that the adult-created problems cannot be worked through or remedied. If this is the case, then our gifted Latinx English language learners and other culturally linguistically diverse gifted learners are facing systemic racism that must be disrupted.

Another piece of the strategic plan for programming is to develop a strategy for gifted Latinx English language learners to access and thrive in culturally responsive curricula, talent development models, and access to advanced academic classes such as Advanced Placement (AP), International Baccalaureate (IB), Honors, and concurrent enrollment. These classes are of importance because, historically, culturally linguistically diverse learners—including English language learners—are not afforded the opportunity to participate in these types of rigorous coursework, yet white, affluent English-speaking learners typically have access and achieve levels of success.

Curriculum considerations must also be taken into account, such as the inclusion of Latinx authors and characters as well as authentic real-world problems in programming for gifted Latinx English language learners. The curriculum materials chosen should represent the learners and incorporate the values of their culture, while being rigorous and at a sufficiently high level. The curriculum should also include matters of social justice for the Latinx community or the student's immediate community. These real-world problems should be incorporated in the curriculum, regardless of the content or the student's language proficiency.

Asking learners to grapple with real-world problems and concept-based curriculum is one of the most appropriate ways to engage gifted Latinx English language learners in learning. Therefore, the authors support the use of concept-based curriculum, as they have used this model with gifted Latinx English language learners themselves. Concept-based curriculum aligns with brain research related to pattern-seeking, and to constructivist and rigorous thinking. A concept-based curriculum model is appropriate for levels of language acquisition because concepts such as power, interdependence, identity, systems, order, structure, and communication exist within and across all languages. Using a concept-based curriculum model allows students to use analogous and deductive reasoning, and forces them to think deeply and make connections across subjects about abstract ideas. It is more than just a regurgitation of facts and basic knowledge; instead, it causes learners to think deeply and critically and can easily be related to the learners' cultural and community values (Erickson & Lanning, 2014). In order for a school district, or even a school itself, to utilize a concept-based curriculum for its gifted Latinx English language learners, educators must have professional learning and engage in concept-based units. They must also have time to plan for this shift away from traditional curriculum and curricular models. As former teachers, the authors have used concept-based curriculum units with their learners and have seen their gifted Latinx English language learners gain independence, think deeply, and engage more with the units. In teaching this concept to other teachers, the authors have seen the teachers think deeply and grapple with concepts that they were excited to take back to their classrooms.

Another consideration for the strategic plan and a critical element in programming is providing access to and opportunity to implement rigorous coursework that is typically available in a secondary setting and allows students to think about post-secondary success. That is, the plan must include a path for students to access and thrive in AP classes, IB classes, Honors classes, and in concurrent enrollment. Additionally, the plan must do more than just offer classes to gifted Latinx English language learners and other culturally linguistically diverse learners. It must include a viable path early, with appropriate scaffolds for language and/or ability prior to high school. If this is not implemented, then learners will not be successful.

In attempting to close the gap and bring equitable access to culturally linguistically diverse learners, there have been district-wide movements such as AP for All (College Board, 2019) in New York City Schools, where a substantial effort was made to bring advanced placement classes to culturally and linguistically diverse high school students. Prior to the 2016 initiative, over 40,000 high school students did not have an option to engage in AP classes and potentially earn college credits. When the initiative was put in place, the number of AP classes offered increased. However, there were large disparities in participation rate and performance of Black and Hispanic students, English language learners, and students with disabilities. Those disparities continue to exist. School districts across the country, including in Florida, Colorado, and California, are also implementing AP, IB, and even Honors for All programming so that culturally linguistically diverse learners have access to rigorous programming. The idea of offering these types of classes for all students to engage in sounds inclusionary and is definitely a goal worth setting; however, without the proper scaffolding, continued language supports, or exposure to these types of classes and thinking beginning in elementary and middle school, the pass rates of culturally linguistically diverse learners will continue to remain low. In the authors' professional experience, the access to rigorous coursework and critical thinking does not happen early enough in the learner's school career. Therefore, in order for gifted Latinx English language learners and other culturally linguistically diverse learners to participate in these classes in high school, vertical teaming with elementary and middle school grade levels to offer access earlier and create a path will better prepare the students to truly engage in the content. There must be a district-wide strategy.

There is a difference between offering a class and accessing the information in that class. Simply having an AP, IB, Honors, or concurrent enrollment class and increasing the numbers of culturally linguistically diverse learners who enroll in it do not mean students have been prepared academically to truly access the content. Once again, by not having a vertical progression of opportunities to engage in rigorous coursework in elementary and middle school, the system is oppressing gifted Latinx English language learners and other culturally linguistically diverse groups of learners.

As stated earlier, access to advanced coursework should happen early and should have linguistic support for gifted Latinx English language learners; however, there are no AP classes or concurrent enrollment in elementary school. Yet learners still must be exposed to the prerequisite thinking and skills needed to access that content, and that can happen through talent development. In a talent development model for learning, student strengths and interests are explored while students are exposed to instructional practices in gifted education that will help them acquire new learning. The authors are advocating for schools and school districts to adopt a talent development model for all learners to provide access and opportunity, and scaffolded linguistic and/or academic support to increase positive academic and social emotional outcomes.

The authors use the term "talent development" as a broad program descriptor where gifted Latinx English language learners are able to access advanced and complex material in an area of relative strength. Talent development, while best supported within the general education classroom and adopted throughout the entire school day, can be part of a continuum of advanced programming in which students engage through pull-out, push-in, independent, and small-group work. In many ways, this is a traditional version of gifted programming; however, in talent development models, all learners receive gifted instruction regardless of identification and all educators are taught the principles of gifted instruction and culturally responsive pedagogy. The authors know that this type of programming is successful for all learners, not just gifted Latinx English language learners. When adopting this type of model, the authors have seen individual schools' academic scores increase across all demographic groups, as well as considerable growth in student engagement and educator satisfaction. With talent development, however, there are mindset shifts that must take place, and there must be an investment in teacher training and professional learning with ongoing coaching and accountability systems in place to support educators and their learners. Launching a talent development model for an entire school may take two years to plan, research, train educators, and work on mindsets in the building. The work on mindsets and instructional practices is ongoing and there must be a plan to onboard new teachers every year. This work is transformational and must be given three years minimum to begin to show positive outcomes. The authors know talent development and transformational change are possible because they have been part of the creative construction of such a model and know the components necessary for success.

The final pieces of the plan for programming are enrichment and social emotional learning opportunities. Enrichment opportunities for gifted Latinx English language learners should allow them to engage in problem-solving, serving their community and exploring their interests that may or may not align with academic objectives, but that instead engage a student in their area of passion (or help them to find one). In addition to academic clubs and groups, the authors encourage enrichment that focuses on student leadership, creativity, and talent areas.

Enrichment could come in the form of the schoolwide enrichment model (Renzulli & Renzulli, 2010), in which school faculty and members of the community teach learners about their own interests, passions, and talents, to which students may not have been exposed. For example, an educator may have a passion for cake decorating or crochet, and wants to teach their love for something that is not traditionally academic to any learners (multiage groups) who are also interested in the same areas. In the schoolwide enrichment model, community members also participate by coming to the school for several weeks and engaging learners in a variety of activities. For example, schoolwide enrichment classes could include opportunities like how to dance ballet folklórico, weave patterns and create clothing and other textile arts, play chess, code video games, create anime, use investigative journalism, explore space, play the harp, and so much more. It is important that any enrichment offered be inclusive of the learners' interests, strengths, and culture, and reflect the community. Operational considerations that must be built into the strategic programming plan should involve the community by planning and discovering community strengths; take into account in-school scheduling considerations (when and how); and include language support across a variety of enrichment opportunities.

Social emotional programming must also be included in culturally responsive gifted programming. Hosting social emotional groups in the heritage language is often missing from gifted education programs across the country. Gifted Latinx English language learners have the same social emotional needs and intensities as their English language peers, and should have a way to process those intensities and emotions. There are multiple avenues to engage gifted Latinx English language learners both socially and emotionally. One avenue, bibliotherapy, has been a well-researched and timeless social emotional support and intervention. As educators and administrators, the authors continue to use bibliotherapy with all their learners (both students and staff). Using books with Latinx characters—ideally gifted Latinx English language learners, which are available in both Spanish and English—will encompass the greatest number of learners possible. Using books that focus on social emotional concerns such as friendship, identity development, anxiety (and countless other topics) that the gifted Latinx English language learners in class are experiencing can help them to process their emotions. It also provides an opportunity for the gifted Latinx English language learner with a window into themselves.

One last social emotional component that crosses into enrichment and academics is mentors and mentorships. Gifted Latinx English language learners can greatly benefit from having a mentor with whom to speak. The purpose of the mentorship can be varied: there might be a need for a career mentorship that exposes the learner to a future job or career; there might be a need for a positive mentor who is older than the mentee to support identity development throughout middle school or high school; the mentor could also serve as purely a social emotional support who has similar interest to the gifted Latinx English language learner and therefore can engage in activities of interest to the learner (basketball, counseling, community activism, etc.). In one example of mentorship, the authors have supported pairing gifted Latinx English language learners with volunteers from a local church group that had ties to the community and that wanted to help the learners form positive and healthy relationships with other people. These mentors came to the school weekly and played chess and other board games with the learners, speaking Spanish with them; they had students opening up to them and sharing details, concerns, and worries as well as joys that they experienced daily. By having mentors who were active in the community, but who were not tied to academics, the gifted Latinx English language learners had an opportunity to relax and be themselves. They also had the opportunity, through some structured and unstructured play, to practice speaking in both English and Spanish. The mentorships can and did change lives. For mentorships and social emotional programming to be a part of the overall strategic plan, education professionals must allocate resources, time, and funds, and have a belief that social emotional learning is important to the development of the whole child. Additionally, linguistic scaffolds must remain in place so the gifted Latinx English language learner can access the appropriate supports.

To summarize, when implementing culturally responsive gifted programming:

- ♦ Develop a strategic plan for programming that considers the time, resources, funding, scheduling needs, and intellectual and emotional shifts in mindset that must occur to implement programming.
- ♦ Use culturally responsive gifted instructional practices:
  - ♦ Include critical and creative thinking.
  - ♦ Include social justice concepts and topics.

- Develop critical and creative thinking through specific questioning.
- Incorporate the values of the students' cultures into the classroom beyond heroes and holidays.
- Include issues of social justice within the students' community.
- Ensure curriculum and planned experiences explore the accomplishments and successes of Latinx people as well as the struggles that the Latinx community has faced and continues to face.
- Provide true access to advanced coursework by having a comprehensive vertical professional and continuum of services.
- Include talent development models when possible.
- Use research-based acceleration processes for content, subject, and grade-level acceleration, regardless of language proficiency.
- Provide scaffolds using advanced language structures to help build English acquisition skills (regardless of grade level or acceleration need).
- Consider using a research-based grouping model such as the schoolwide cluster grouping model to support positive academic and social emotional outcomes and increase student growth.
- Ensure gifted Latinx English language learners have access to culturally responsive enrichment opportunities.
    - The schoolwide enrichment model based on student interest and passions can occur during the day.
    - Include opportunities in heritage language.
    - Ensure opportunities exist to engage in complex and creative problem-solving.
    - Use technology to bring opportunities to students.
- Include social emotional learning:
    - Create a classroom library (with audio and print books) written by Latinx authors where gifted Latinx learners are the protagonists and heroes.
    - Utilize mirror books that have characters who are navigating anxiety, depression, perfectionism,

underachievement, twice exceptionality, synchrony, and so on as part of the curriculum.
- ♦ Provide mentors and mentorships with the school's local and greater Latinx community so students may have opportunity to see leadership, career opportunities, and the path needed to work in an area of passion.
- ♦ Connect local community resources to families and bring those local resources into the school setting.

Professional Learning

A key piece of the DuBois Greene Culturally Responsive Gifted Framework that is essential to culturally responsive gifted education is professional learning, particularly its role in supporting educators and students. The term "professional development" does not encapsulate what the authors advocate for: professional learning that is active and transformational, and that challenges deeply held assumptions and traditional ways of knowing (Kegan, 2000). Instead the authors challenge their readers to push beyond information learning and move adult learners into transformational learning, which changes how a person knows (Drago-Severson, 2009) and understands the work in front of them. Specifically, transformational learning changes the structure of educators' meaning-making and construction of meaning. Transformational learning is active, evolving, self-reflective, and perspective taking; it exemplifies the elements of culturally responsive pedagogy.

As explored in Chapter 5, a culturally responsive gifted professional creates the classroom conditions necessary to support the academic and social emotional needs of their gifted Latinx English language learners. That is, educators must be willing to embark on a journey that includes learning and incorporating research-based gifted instructional practices and programming, and programming supported by gifted education and culturally responsive education. The authors are advocating for the development of culturally responsive gifted professionals through four specific areas of individualized and specific areas of professional learning: educator mindsets, culturally responsive professional learning, gifted professional learning, and reflection on practice.

When thinking about the role played by professional learning in the DuBois Greene Culturally Responsive Gifted Framework, it is important to remember the needs of a culturally responsive gifted classroom because such a classroom is explicitly connected to a culturally responsive gifted educator. The two are so interdependent that it can be difficult to decide which section of learning should come before the other. Again, schools cannot have successful culturally responsive gifted classrooms and programming if the educator with whom the learners engage is not a culturally responsive gifted professional themselves. Therefore, based on research and their own professional experiences, the authors have identified the key components of a strategic professional learning plan.

The first step in cultivation requires the school district or individual school to create a strategic plan for professional learning. Since the learning is centered around culturally and linguistically supportive instructional practices, the authors recommend that, when possible, the development of this professional learning plan should involve multiple stakeholders in the district or school who have a specific content expertise. The plan must have clearly stated objectives that anchor the entire learning experience, as well as several mini-objectives that inform realistic and attainable outcomes. These goals/objectives should be SMART (Specific, Measurable, Achievable/Attainable, Realistic, and Time bound) in nature.

The overarching objective should be built on equitable practices, and focus on creating an environment that disrupts structural and internalized systems of oppression. In order to do this, a school and/or school district must be given time to engage in professional learning cycles in which educators are able to take risks, make mistakes and learn from them, engage in purposeful learning, experience cognitive dissonance, and construct meaning for themselves. The strategic plan for development will be multi-year (possibly two to three years) in implementation and will need time to demonstrate success based on what the district determines as success. Finally, this strategic plan should link directly to student outcomes. Therefore, when developing the plan for professional learning, school district leaders or school administrators should name the specific student outcomes they expect to occur (i.e. increase student engagement, increase family engagement, positive assessment score attribution).

As logistical planning is underway, it is critical to think about the process of learning and engagement. It is therefore important to ensure that the professional learning is authentic, job-embedded, focused on principles of andragogy (the science of adult learning), and self-directed (Merriam, 2001). Job-embedded professional learning is important to professional learning because it shows "promise as an approach that accommodates teachers' varying levels of knowledge and experience in preparing them to meet the diverse needs of their students" (Cavazos, Linan-Thompson, & Ortiz, 2018). Job embedded professional learning is an effective way to support educators and their preference for engaging with learning and applying new understandings. It is a form of professional learning that has been embraced and studied by those in the field of education, and is one of the preferred methods of obtaining and retaining learning. In addition to this consideration, the facilitator(s) must also determine the modality for engaging adults and consider the use of technology and distance learning when appropriate. Consider the use of book studies and affinity groups.

Once the initial logistical considerations of when and how professional learning and learning will occur are established, the next portion of the strategic plan should consider the content and its scope and sequence. As stated earlier, there are four large and comprehensive topics that create the content through which educators will engage. These include educator mindsets, culturally responsive professional learning (including the support of linguistic diversity), gifted professional learning, and reflection on practice. Chapter 5 explored the different components of these topics in greater, although not complete, detail. The following section is a suggested professional learning road map based on the authors' experiences in the creation of professional learning for culturally responsive gifted education professionals. It can also be used with paraprofessionals, school psychologists, counselors, social workers, families, community members, and students. The authors have tried culturally responsive professional learning in a variety of ways and in various iterations within their own careers. Figure 8.2 shows a suggested order and overarching topics of study.

Additional considerations for professional learning include ensuring that appropriate systems and structures are in place to sustain learning. This can come in the form of developing an

Professional Learning Roadmap	
Year One Suggested Order of Topics	Years Two and Three Suggested Order of Topics
Dismantling Systems of Oppression: Begin with Self	Dismantling Systems of Oppression: Students, Families, and Culturally Responsive Gifted Education
Exploring Mindsets	Culturally Responsive Gifted Education
The Educator's Personal Cultural Identity	Cultures in the Classroom and the Community
The Role of Privilege	Seeing and Recognizing Giftedness
White Supremacy Culture and Systemic Racism	Gifted Instructional and Programming Practices
Critical Conversations about Race	Family Engagement
Tips for Impacting and Sustaining Learning *These tips are not meant to be weekly topics, as these subjects require time and attention. All learning and ongoing work must be job-embedded.* • Establish working agreements, including a space for non-judgement • Establish working agreements around self-regulation and staying in the zone of tolerance • Embody theories of adult learning and is culturally responsive. • Include continuous reflection through multiple means of expression or demonstration • Build in reflection into staff coaching, teacher planning/committees, and in observations • Include action items and next steps as well as periodically evaluate the impact of learning	

FIGURE 8.2
Professional learning roadmap

onboarding process or running multiple professional learning series simultaneously based on the needs of educators. It includes a plan for educators to become facilitators of learning by strategically building their capacity. Sustainable systems will also include an identified structure for incorporating the learning into administrator and teacher observations, coaching conversations, and as part of the school's overall plan, vision, and mission.

Professional learning—adult learning—should not be static. Instead, it should be responsive to the adults' needs and assessed continually. At the end of every session, or before moving on to the next study, mini-evaluations should occur, asking about facilitation, topics, and needs. The answers to these questions will impact both the scope and sequence of the professional learning for the year. Because of their complex nature, it is expected that some concepts will take multiple weeks to explore. Within each of these major topics are sub-topics to delve into, and facilitation will need to adapt to help learners actively construct meaning and push through any cognitive dissonance they may be experiencing.

As part of the professional learning evaluation, include at least one social emotional question about how the participants are feeling and what next steps they will take to internalize and make sense of the learning. In professional learning, prioritizing the social emotional and intellectual wellbeing of adult learners is critical for them to feel safe, to trust one another, and to be in a place where they can learn.

This professional learning road map is not easily traversed, and does not have to be traveled alone. If it were a topographical map, it would show many natural barriers to a destination, such as mountains, plateaus, and rivers, necessitating a series of course corrections. This is internalized oppression, manifested as microaggressions and implicit bias. The roadmap would also show human-created barriers such as bridges, buildings, and houses that represent human-made laws, policies, structures, and systems that support systemic and structural racism. One must understand, however, that these artificial or naturally occurring barriers are not permanent. They can be torn down and built back up in the form of bridges to understanding.

As educators engage in this journey and travel using this roadmap, remember that there are caution signs. Engaging in critical conversations about race, privilege, identity, and systemic racism is necessary, and must be done with careful thought and consideration because if it is not done appropriately, with agreed-upon working arrangements and trust, then there is a risk of trauma and damaged relationships. However, if these issues are not confronted, then there is the risk of continued trauma and damaged relationships, not only to the adults participating, but also to the learners in their classrooms and the families they support.

Developing a culturally responsive gifted professionals takes time, investment, and commitment from all involved, including district and school level entities. This helps to fracture and dismantle the systems of oppression that gifted Latinx English language learners face. By impacting mindsets in adults, we can impact self-worth and efficacy in children.

To summarize, when creating professional learning that cultivates culturally responsive gifted professionals, ensure the following:

- Develop a multi-year job-embedded professional learning and implementation plan.
- Use best practices in adult learning theory to engage adults.
- Demonstrate understanding of key learnings by engaging in critical conversations around race and language outside the structured professional learning.
- Include a plan to onboard new educators so that they have access to the information in a timely manner.
- Keep race and language at the center of learning.
- Explore the critical roles of educators' mindsets and implicit bias.
- Ensure that educators have an understanding of culturally responsive education, gifted education, and culturally responsive gifted practices.
- Give educators the opportunity to fail forward and learn from any missteps.

♦ Sustain learning by including essential understandings in feedback and coaching sessions as well as in classroom observation protocols.
♦ Use ongoing reflection to for process improvement.

Family Engagement

The final component in the DuBois Greene Culturally Responsive Gifted Framework is family engagement—specifically, a family and community partnership. A strong relationship between families, community partners, and the school or district is essential for the overall success of gifted Latinx English language learners and their families. This partnership has the potential to help recruit, retain, and support the whole child. As in previous sections, it is imperative for a school district and individual schools to develop, review, or modify a culturally responsive plan to engage families.

When beginning a strategic plan for family engagement, remember to define the purpose of family engagement, and encourage the use of the inclusive term "family" to supplant the term "parent." Families are multidimensional, and in the Latinx community in the United States they may even live in multigenerational households or near each other in the same community.

The purpose of family engagement should align with the overarching goals of the gifted program, and can be strengthened when connected with the other components of the DuBois Greene Culturally Responsive Gifted Framework. In deciding the purpose, ask the following questions:

1. Is the purpose of family engagement to distribute information and promote a program?
2. Is the purpose of family engagement to inform families about identification, assessment, and programming?
3. Is the purpose of family engagement to develop a partnership with families to inform practice and policies?
4. Is the purpose of family engagement to create opportunities for families to give feedback to district administration or school administration?

5. Is the purpose of family engagement any combination of the above questions?
6. What implicit biases about Latinx families and English language learners need to be processed and dismantled before engaging with families?

Family engagement and community partnership serve as essential lifelines and sources of support for gifted education, programming, policies, identification practices, and advocacy. However, although a piece of family engagement will involve informative sessions designed to help families understand identification practices, characteristics and needs, as well as programming and support tools, information-giving should not be the sole purpose of family engagement.

Instead, the authors advocate a comprehensive family engagement plan—one that is co-constructed with the families and sees them as experts regarding their children. It is a plan that asks families for feedback about programming, communication, and school district practices and policies. It sees the educator as an active participant in sharing knowledge about gifted practices and social emotional support, while learning what the family needs and how to best support gifted Latinx English language learners. At the very minimum, family engagement and community partnership should support gifted Latinx English language learners in their school career and post-secondary journey by identifying more gifted Latinx English language learners who are in-service English language learners, as well as those students who have exited from a language program and creating a positive and culturally responsive gifted classroom environment.

When working on the plan, remember to include any information, applications, notes, phone calls, text messages, or emails in the heritage language. If the educator is a non-Spanish speaking individual, then the strategic plan must have considerations for reducing the linguistic barriers for both the family and the educators by having interpreters and using translation software or devices to communicate. If possible, have an English interpreter instead of only Spanish interpreters for the educator engaging in a family–teacher conference, and host an information night or family fun night in Spanish only.

If the plan's purpose is to have families provide guidance on identification practices that impact gifted Latinx English language learners, then any school district or school policy/practice must be available for review in the heritage language. Families can be asked to give feedback, either verbal or written, in their heritage language, and the education professionals can then engage in a conversation and potentially make changes to documents, practices, and policies. Or families can engage in a conversation with the educator or administrator in a more casual manner and share their feedback. The goal of the educator and administrator is to listen to the families and try to determine the impact on them of policies, practices, and communication.

The most powerful family engagement the authors have witnessed is families supporting families. Whether family engagement is a board game night or a night grounded in helping their children become stronger critical thinkers, the more tools that can be given to families to help them talk with one another about navigating systems or understanding characteristics of giftedness, the better our identification will be because families will become more aware of giftedness. Conversely, the more educators listen to the strengths of the learner based on their family's perception, the stronger identification also becomes because educators are able to see giftedness that may otherwise have gone unrecognized.

When possible, a home visit is an appropriate way to build a relationship with students and their families—that is, provided the families have had enough time to invite the educator into the house or have time available to meet. During the home visit, the educator or administrator is there to learn about the gifted Latinx English language outside of a typical school setting. In Chapter 6, as well as in Appendix G, the authors have shared an example of a family questionnaire that can be used to facilitate a conversation with families. Families must not feel as if they are being interrogated. Instead, this must be a fluid conversation with them about their child. Remember, many of our culturally linguistically diverse families, including our Latinx

English language learning families, have been disenfranchised by the school system or may be uncomfortable with a home visit and numerous questions. Therefore, ensure the tone is conversational in style. If the family cannot meet in person, then consider other modalities such as a phone call or tele-distance conversation via the internet. If the internet is not available for the learner or the learner does not have a phone, work with the family to determine when you can connect and how. It may be that the educator has to meet the family at a neutral location within the community chosen by the family. This, too, is completely appropriate because the goal in completing home–school visits is to build trust.

An additional key component of working with families is the role of the community. Community members may see gifted Latinx English language learners in a different way to those at home or at school. Therefore, it is important to include community members as people who are able to refer a child or even help provide education to families. When including community members, remember to offer informational sessions on the characteristics of gifted Latinx learners and social emotional needs. Also share how to navigate the school system and help them understand characteristics as well as social emotional supports. Ask community members what they value as strengths and how they think the school community should interact and engage with them.

The authors have learned the importance of location to family engagement opportunities. When possible, such opportunities should occur in a location other than the school building or district-level office. There are multiple hidden messages and power dynamics that are implicitly understood or communicated on the basis of where and how families are engaged. Holding family engagement events and sessions in the community is a way to set up a known and safe space for families, so the authors suggest working with the community partners to host family engagement opportunities at their facility. For example, hosting an engagement within the community center or at the local library within the community brings the opportunity to the families. When the authors have gone into the community to hand out flyers, hold events, and engage in listening sessions at family-owned establishments, Latinx-owned and operated businesses, churches, recreation centers, libraries and so on, the number of families who are communicated with and who come to events increases.

Leaning on the community as an additional support for identification, enrichment, and programming can further enrich the lives of gifted Latinx English language learners. By engaging the community, the school and/or district is sending the message that one community as a whole will support, watch over, and care for this very important population of neurodivergent learners.

To summarize, when supporting family engagement, educators and administrators should include, but not limit themselves to, the following:

- Develop, review, or modify a strategic plan for family engagement and community partnerships.
- All communication and correspondence must be in the heritage language as well as the host language:
    - Include letters, websites, emails, newsletters, phone calls, and fliers.
    - Ensure that equal linguistic attention is paid to both the heritage and the host languages.
- Create opportunities for families to review, give feedback, and share their perspectives on programming, communication, and gifted identification practices.
- Have conversation-style community events in the heritage language, with English interpretation available if needed.
- Develop a Latinx family council to help inform decisions and provide feedback.
- Build the capacity of the Latinx family council to inform the community and other Latinx families about gifted Latinx English language learners and their needs, and help them to navigate systems.
- Engage the community to help identify gifted learners.
- Hold regular listening sessions to understand the needs of the community.
- Ensure childcare is available. If not, ensure there are activities for children to engage in near their families.
- When possible, feed families or offer snacks.

A Call to Action

Gifted Latinx English language learners have extraordinary gifts, talents, and qualitatively different needs from their neurotypical peers—needs that are often overlooked and underserved. In studying trends and schools around the United States, the National Center for Research on Gifted Education noted the difficulty in identifying gifted English language learners and the complexities that come with recognizing the strengths of a learner in their heritage language (Mun et al., 2016). However, additional research supports the authors' experience and shows that with specific practices, gifted Latinx English language learners are able to be identified and receive services. The researchers determined that the following specific practices improved identification of learners and align with the DuBois Greene Culturally Responsive Gifted Framework: adopt a universal assessment; include alternative pathways to identification; establish communication understanding; and use of professional learning to help drive change and improvement (Gubbins et. al., 2020). Data related to increased identification and supports of gifted Latinx English language learners are promising; however, it will take time to shift the narrative.

Educators and administrators must actively dismantle the systems of oppression that are in place at the national, state, and local levels of education. To truly transform gifted education, a combination of technical and adaptive (Heifetz & Laurie, 2001) changes is necessary for the field. Some are more technical changes to guidelines, schedules, and rules guiding practice. These problems can be solved by experts and have a clear solution. Most of the required changes, however, are mindset-driven and are what Heifetz and Laurie (2001) term "adaptive changes" because they require new learning. They are complex and need behavioral modification in order to implement the technical changes. Solutions for adaptive changes require new learning and involve stakeholders. Depending on the specific adaptive challenge, stakeholders may include any combination of the following: community members, educators, family members, students, administrators, and law-makers.

It is educational malfeasance to continue the exclusionary practices observed in gifted education programs across the country. Many states and local school districts have not only recognized the systemic inequities that exist for gifted Latinx English language learners, but are actively working to disrupt a century of racism in gifted education. In order to do this work, there must be some local, state, and/or national level policy recommendation and changes that are both adaptive and technical in nature.

Recommendations

The National Association of Gifted Children (2020) states that, "Although Federal law acknowledges that children with gifts and talents have unique needs that are not traditionally offered in regular school settings, it offers no specific provisions, mandates, or requirements for serving these children." In the absence of a federal law that mandates identification and programming for gifted learners, gifted education has become a mosaic of state and local approaches with different definitions of giftedness, varying and inconsistent standards for programming and professional learning, and inconsistent standards related to state-level funding. This perpetuates the myth that gifted learners will be fine and keeps systems of oppression in place because gifted education is consistently available only to those who can afford it.

Unlike special education, gifted education is also not funded at the federal level and, as mentioned previously, there are inconsistencies in standards related to state funding—if state funding exists. For traditionally marginalized populations, such as gifted Latinx English language learners and gifted learners in general, the absence of law, policy, and/or clear district practice continues to construct barriers to access. The implied value statements that can be discerned from lack of investment in our nation's most promising learners are unacceptable. In addition to the research-based and experience-based changes for which the authors have advocated through this book, additional suggestions have been developed for changes at the district and state levels to change the narrative:

1. Develop a compelling vision framed in social justice and civil rights for gifted Latinx English language learners and all gifted culturally diverse learners.
2. Develop an expanded definition of giftedness to include bilingualism and include language in district and state level documents, policies, and if possible state legislation.
3. Develop a common definition of equity created with multiple stakeholders with diverse perspectives, and communicate that message broadly.
4. Leverage the local school board to help communicate this message of equity and request a resolution naming the definition and a commitment to gifted culturally linguistically diverse learners.
5. Develop and implement an inclusive acceleration policy for NEP, LEP, and FEP learners that allows for subject and grade level acceleration regardless of English proficiency. Next, codify the statement by creating school board policy.
6. Codify policy.
7. Work with Human Resources to help create a district-level policy that will recruit and retain bilingual Latinx educators who are trained in gifted education, or who are willing to be trained in gifted education.
8. Include a minimum of continuing education hours in culturally linguistically diverse education as well as gifted education for all educators who are renewing their licenses.
9. Universities should include culturally responsive gifted education into the minimum requirements for pre-service educators (or separate classes on both).
10. Universities should include culturally responsive gifted education into the minimum requirements for undergraduate studies for pre-service teachers and administrators (or separate classes on both).

11. In states that do not have inclusive language or legislation related to gifted education, work with local advocacy groups and lawmakers to discuss legislation.
12. Identification policies at the local and state level should include local and group-specific norms, multiple pathways for identification, talent development as a pathway towards identification, and the use of alternative assessment measures to support placement in gifted programs.
13. District and local school plans should identify a specific culturally responsive gifted programming plan for gifted Latinx English language learners and embed it into their accountability systems.
14. Establish working groups within the district between the gifted department and the English language department, if those departments exist. If they do not exist at the district level, inquire into how the two departments are connecting at the state level to support different learners and their educators.
15. Work with the administrator supporting TITLE funds to discuss the use of TITLE III funds being used to support gifted professional learning (remember there is no mandate, but funds can be used in this manner).
16. Advocate for a fully funded mandate for gifted education with the state department. Work with the National Association for Gifted Children to develop this type of leadership and advocacy lens.
17. Through awareness of the problem, educators (and legislators) can act to:
    ♦ ensure that all schools identify students with gifts and talents from underrepresented populations
    ♦ put into place equitable identification procedures and programming designed to develop and reveal talents among all children, and especially those that have been underserved for generations.

Next Steps in Transformational Change

A note to district administrators: what systems need to be in place to ensure that we don't lose kids? What identification practices does your district have that help learners be identified or hinder this process? What about your policies around acceleration? Are the social emotional supports in place to help transition learners? What about mentorships?

Once educators actively begin exploring the role of culture (race and language), and keeping race at the center of their professional learning, questioning implicit bias and microaggressions, the next step is to begin reviewing your policies and practices within your school and district that perpetuate or disrupt systems of oppression for all gifted Latinx English language learners as well as with all gifted culturally linguistically diverse gifted learners.

The act of looking at gifted policies with a critical eye is what Greene (2017) refers to as GiftedCrit, or Gifted Critical Race Theory. Like DisCrit, and Indigenous Crit, GiftedCrit has evolved from the original theories of Critical Race Theory (Jay, 2003; Ladson-Billings, 1998) and is applied to the systemic and structural racism that exists within gifted education. Using components of the theory to explore policies and practices is the next step in transformation and razing systems of oppression.

Educators in the field must ask whether the lives of gifted Latinx English language learners are important enough to injure the system badly enough so that it cannot return to its original state. This is not easy, and it will take years to change. The late novelist, playwright, and social activist James Baldwin famously stated, "Not everything that is faced can be changed. But nothing can be changed until it is faced." It is time to truly face what has been in front of educators for a very long time and commit to change.

References

Assouline, S. G., Colangelo, N., Lupkowski-Shoplik, A., Forstadt, L., & Lipscomb, J. (2020). *Iowa Acceleration Scale manual: a guide for whole-grade acceleration K-8*. Kansas, MI: Gifted Unlimited.

Brulles, D., Peters, S. J., & Saunders, R. (2012). Schoolwide mathematics achievement within the gifted cluster grouping model. *Journal of Advanced Academics, 23*(3), 200–216.

Brulles, D., Saunders, R., & Cohn, S. J. (2010). Improving performance for gifted students in a cluster grouping model. *Journal for the Education of the Gifted, 34*(2), 327–350.

Brulles, D., & Winebrenner, S. (2011). The schoolwide cluster grouping model: Restructuring gifted education services for the 21st century. *Gifted Child Today, 34*(4), 35–46.

Castellano, J. (1998). Identifying and assessing gifted and talented bilingual Hispanic students. Retrieved October 1, 2020, from https://www.davidsongifted.org/search-database/entry/a10362

Cavazos, L., Linan-Thompson, S., & Ortiz, A. (2018). Job-embedded professional development for teachers of English learners: Preventing literacy difficulties through effective core instruction. *Teacher Education and Special Education, 41*(3), 203–214.

College Board (2019, September 20). AP for all—NYC: Education professional. Retrieved October 1, 2020, from https://professionals.collegeboard.org/testing/states-local-governments/partnerships/nyc/ap-all

Drago-Severson, E. (2009). *Leading adult learning: Supporting adult development in our schools.* Thousand Oaks, CA: Corwin Press.

Erickson, H. L., & Lanning, L. A. (2014). *Transitioning to concept-based curriculum and instruction: How to bring content and process together.* Thousand Oaks, CA: Corwin Press.

Great Schools Partnership (2016). The glossary of education reform. Retrieved September 20, 2020, from www.edglossary.org/21st-century-skills

Greene, R. M. (2017). Gifted culturally linguistically diverse learners: A school-based Exploration. Unpublished doctoral dissertation, University of Denver, Denver, CO.

Gubbins, E. J., Siegle, D., Peters, P. M., Carpenter, A. Y., Hamilton, R., McCoach, D. B., Puryear, J. S., Langley, S. D., & Long, D. (2020). Promising practices for improving identification of English learners for gifted and talented programs. *Journal for the Education of the Gifted, 43*(4), 336–369.

Heifetz, R. A., & Laurie, D. L. (2001). The work of leadership. *Harvard Business Review, 79*(11), 124–134.

Jay, M. (2003). Critical race theory, multicultural education, and the hidden curriculum of hegemony. *Multicultural Perspectives: An Official Journal of the National Association for Multicultural Education, 5*(4), 3–9.

Kagan, R. (2000). What "form" transforms? A constructive-developmental approach to transformative learning. In J. Mezirow & Associates (Eds.), *Learning as transformation* (pp. 35–70). San Francisco: Jossey-Bass.

Ladson-Billings, G. (1998). Just what is critical race theory and what's it doing in a nice field like education? *International Journal of Qualitative Studies in Education, 11*(1), 7–24.

Matthews, M. S., Ritchotte, J. A., & McBee, M. T. (2013). Effects of schoolwide cluster grouping and within-class ability grouping on elementary school students' academic achievement growth. *High Ability Studies, 24*(2), 81–97.

Merriam, S. B. (2001). Andragogy and self-directed learning: Pillars of adult learning theory. *New Directions for Adult and Continuing Education, 89*, 3–14.

Mun, R. U., Langley, S. D., Ware, S., Gubbins, S. J., Siegle, D., Callahan, C. M., McCoach, B., & Hamilton, R. (2016). *Effective practices for identifying and serving English learners in gifted education: A systematic review of the literature.* Washington, DC: National Center for Research on Gifted Education.

National Association for Gifted Children. (2020). Gifted education in the U.S. Retrieved December 27, 2020 from www.nagc.org/resources-publications/resources/gifted-education-us

Peters, S. J., & Gentry, M. (2012). Group-specific norms and teacher-rating scales: Implications for underrepresentation. *Journal of Advanced Academics, 23*(2), 125–144.

Peters, S. J., Rambo-Hernandez, K., Makel, M. C., Matthews, M. S., & Plucker, J. A. (2019). Effect of local norms on racial and ethnic representation in gifted education. *AERA Open, 5*(2). doi:10.1177/2332858419848446

Renzulli, J. S., & Renzulli, S. R. (2010). The schoolwide enrichment model: A focus on student strengths and interests. *Gifted Education International, 26*(2–3), 140–156. doi:10.1177/026142941002600303

Swanson, J. D. (2006). Breaking through assumptions about low-income, minority gifted students. *Gifted Child Quarterly, 50*(1), 11–25.

Appendix A

DuBois Greene Culturally Responsive Gifted Framework

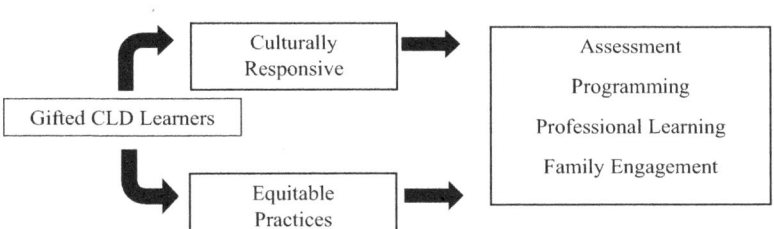

From Michelle Pacheco DuBois and Robin M. Greene, *Supporting gifted ELLs in the Latinx community: Practical strategies*, K–12. New York: Routledge. © 2021.

Appendix B

DuBois Greene Culturally Responsive Gifted Framework: Latinx ELLs

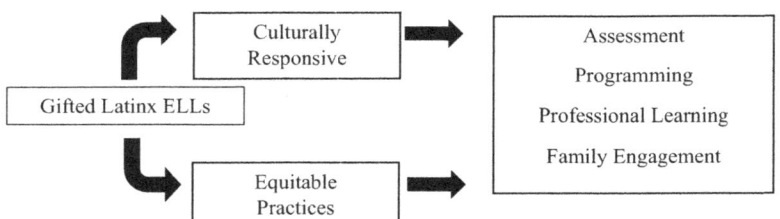

From Michelle Pacheco DuBois and Robin M. Greene, *Supporting gifted ELLs in the Latinx community: Practical strategies, K–12*. New York: Routledge. © 2021.

Appendix C

Greene DuBois Latinx Gifted Behavior Observation Tool

When utilizing the observation tool below, remember that behavior characteristics may have positive and negative manifestations.

Directions

Place a tally mark in the frequency column every time you notice the behavior characteristic compared with the student's native peers. Write a description of the behavior in the observation notes section.

Name: _____ Date of observation(s):_____

Examiner's name: _____ Position: _____

Length of time the examiner has known the student:_____

Behavior Characteristics	Frequency	Observation Notes
Reads 2 or more grade levels above in heritage language		
Rapid second language acquisition		
Superior interpreter abilities *Adjusts tone, style, and register based on the interaction*		

Appendices

Behavior Characteristics	Frequency	Observation Notes
Ability to code switch *Language and affect changes based on environmental situations*		
Easily navigates between cultures *Understands nuances and differences within cultures*		
Asks insightful questions		
Creative ability		
Advanced sense of humor *Understands idiomatic phrases, puns, and jokes in English and Spanish*		
Outstanding math potential or abilities		
Leadership abilities *Positive or negative* *Multiple settings* *With or without native peers*		
Exceptional abilities in fine arts and/or talent		

From Michelle Pacheco DuBois and Robin M. Greene, *Supporting gifted ELLs in the Latinx community: Practical strategies, K–12*. New York: Routledge. © 2021.

This page may be reproduced for individual classrooms or small group work only. For all other uses, contact the authors for permission.

Appendix D
Expanded Body of Evidence

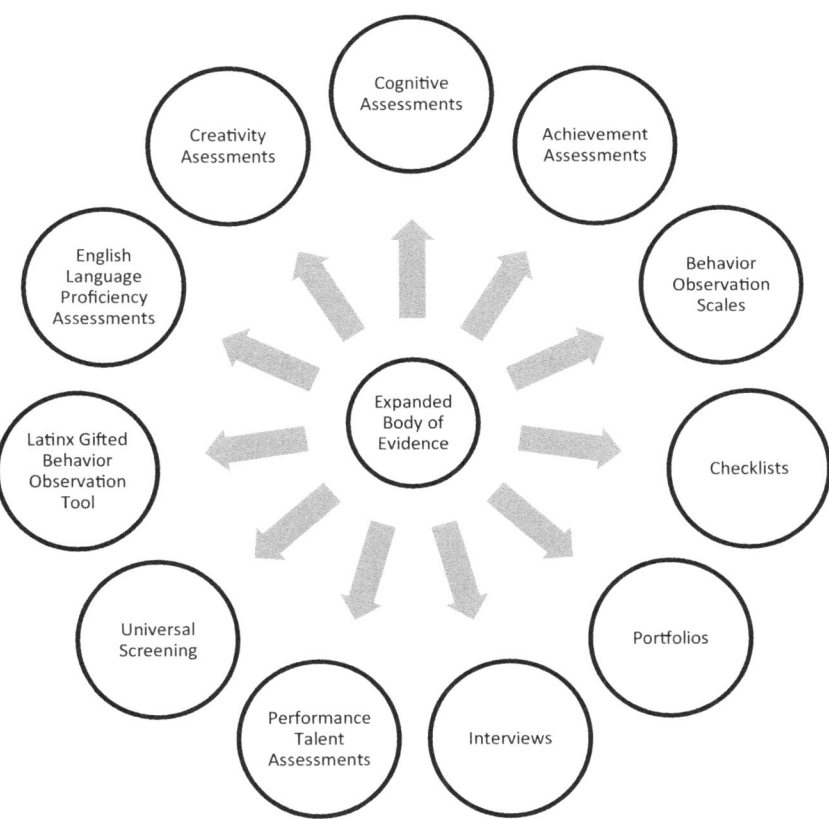

From Michelle Pacheco DuBois and Robin M. Greene, *Supporting gifted ELLs in the Latinx community: Practical strategies, K–12*. New York: Routledge. © 2021.

Appendix E

Student Interview Survey

1. What are you interested in learning about?

2. What causes you frustration?

3. What brings you joy or makes you happy?

4. Who do you trust and why?

5. Is there anything you would change about your learning experience?

6. What do you want people to know about the world?

7. What makes you "you"?

From Michelle Pacheco DuBois and Robin M. Greene, *Supporting gifted ELLs in the Latinx community: Practical strategies, K–12*. New York: Routledge. © 2021.

Appendix F

Encuesta de entrevista estudiantes

1. ¿Qué le interesa aprender?
2. ¿Qué te causa frustración?
3. ¿Qué te trae alegría o te hace feliz?
4. ¿En quién confías y por qué?
5. ¿Hay algo que cambiarías sobre tu experiencia de aprendizaje?
6. ¿Qué quieres que la gente sepa sobre el mundo?
7. ¿Qué te hace "tú"?

From Michelle Pacheco DuBois and Robin M. Greene, *Supporting gifted ELLs in the Latinx community: Practical strategies, K–12*. New York: Routledge. © 2021.

Appendix G

Family Questionnaire

1. What are your child's strengths and interests? What has been challenging?

2. What kind of activities do you like to do together as a family?

3. What kind of activities (read, create games, play sports, etc.) does your child like to do outside of school?

4. What are your hopes and dreams for your child?

5. What kinds of needs or challenges do you have that might prevent your student from participating in enrichment or extension activities?

6. Are there any resources that you need at home (books, materials to support your child's interests, etc.) to support your child?

7. What other things would you like us to know about your child?

From Michelle Pacheco DuBois and Robin M. Greene, *Supporting gifted ELLs in the Latinx community: Practical strategies, K–12*. New York: Routledge. © 2021.

Appendix H
Cuestionario familiar

1. ¿Cuáles son las fortalezas e intereses de su hijo? ¿Qué ha sido un desafío?

2. ¿Qué tipo de actividades les gusta hacer en familia?

3. ¿Qué tipo de actividades (leer, crear juegos, practicar deportes, etc.) le gusta hacer a su hijo fuera de la escuela?

4. ¿Cuáles son sus esperanzas y sueños para su hijo?

5. ¿Qué tipo de necesidades o desafíos tiene que podrían impedir que su estudiante participe en actividades de enriquecimiento o extensión?

6. ¿Hay algún recurso que necesite en casa (libros, materiales para apoyar los intereses de su hijo, etc.) para apoyar a su hijo?

7. ¿Qué otras cosas le gustaría que supiéramos sobre su hijo?

From Michelle Pacheco DuBois and Robin M. Greene, *Supporting gifted ELLs in the Latinx community: Practical strategies, K–12.* New York: Routledge. © 2021.

Appendix I

Body of Evidence and Programming Plan

Student name:	Date(s) of BOE review:
Age:	Language spoken at home:
Grade:	Referred by:
Body of evidence	
Ability/aptitude data:	Achievement data:
School Rating Scale/Observation data:	Home Rating Scale/Observation data:
Student strengths:	**Student interests:**
Gifted and talented programming	
Student engagement:	Family engagement:
Social emotional learning:	Enrichment opportunities:
Community connections:	Other:

From Michelle Pacheco DuBois and Robin M. Greene, *Supporting gifted ELLs in the Latinx community: Practical strategies, K–12*. New York: Routledge. © 2021.

Appendix J
Professional Learning Roadmap

Professional Learning Roadmap	
Year One Suggested Order of Topics	**Years Two and Three** Suggested Order of Topics
Dismantling Systems of Oppression: Begin with Self	Dismantling Systems of Oppression: Students, Families, and Culturally Responsive Gifted Education
Exploring Mindsets	Culturally Responsive Gifted Education
The Educator's Personal Cultural Identity	Cultures in the Classroom and the Community
The Role of Privilege	Seeing and Recognizing Giftedness
White Supremacy Culture and Systemic Racism	Gifted Instructional and Programming Practices
Critical Conversations about Race	Family Engagement
Tips for Impacting and Sustaining Learning *These tips are not meant to be weekly topics, as these subjects require time and attention. All learning and ongoing work must be job-embedded.* • Establish working agreements, including a space for non-judgement • Establish working agreements around self-regulation and staying in the zone of tolerance • Embody theories of adult learning and is culturally responsive. • Include continuous reflection through multiple means of expression or demonstration • Build in reflection into staff coaching, teacher planning/committees, and in observations • Include action items and next steps as well as periodically evaluate the impact of learning	

From Michelle Pacheco DuBois and Robin M. Greene, *Supporting gifted ELLs in the Latinx community: Practical strategies, K–12*. New York: Routledge. © 2021.

Appendix K

Checklist for Culturally Responsive Gifted Best Practices
Latinx ELLs

Assessment
• Are there multiple assessment options that are culture fair? • Are the assessments available in the student's native, or heritage, language? • Does the body of evidence contain both qualitative and quantitative data? • Are there opportunities for students to be universally screened? • Are there performance assessment options for students to demonstrate giftedness in the arts, creativity, and leadership? • Is there an opportunity to demonstrate outstanding performance through academic and/or talent portfolios? • Are language proficiency data reviewed for students demonstrating gifted potential throughout the school year? When and how often are data reviewed? • Is the option to use local norms available? • Are group-specific norm data available to use for either gifted identification or talent development opportunities?
Programming
• Are gifted Latinx ELLs able to see and hear themselves in the curriculum? • How is the heritage language intentionally valued and incorporated? • Do gifted Latinx ELLs have access to advanced linguistic supports? • Are there opportunities for gifted Latinx ELLs to develop critical and creative thinking? • Are Latinx students provided with authentic learning experiences that reflect their native culture?

Programming
• What opportunities exist for gifted Latinx ELLs to access advanced programming and acceleration throughout their school careers? • What available grouping and pacing opportunities exist for advanced academic and social emotional needs? • How do gifted Latinx ELLs participate in advanced programming options such as Advanced Placement, International Baccalaureate, and concurrent enrollment? • Are talent development opportunities provided for gifted Latinx ELLs?
Professional learning
• Does your school district have a strategic plan for developing culturally responsive gifted professionals? • Are there professional learning opportunities for educators and administrators to explore and reflect upon their own cultural identity, including the role of microaggression and implicit bias? • How do educators and administrators actively learn about the values and cultures of their school and classroom community? • Are there gifted education professional learning opportunities for educators and administrators?
Family engagement
• How is information about gifted identification and advanced programming being communicated to Latinx families? • Are Latinx families being given multiple opportunities and ways to engage in conversations with teachers and administrators about their child? Are these conversations asset based? • In what ways are Latinx families engaged in the school community? • In what ways is the school inviting Latinx families in? • How does the school recognize and incorporate the strengths of Latinx families into the classroom? • Is there a partnership with Latinx families and teachers to promote the education of the child?

From Michelle Pacheco DuBois and Robin M. Greene, *Supporting gifted ELLs in the Latinx community: Practical strategies, K–12*. New York: Routledge. © 2021.

Appendix L

Checklist for Culturally Responsive Gifted Best Practices
CLD Learners

Assessment
• Are there multiple assessment options that are culture fair? • Are the assessments available in the student's native, or heritage, language? • Does the body of evidence contain both qualitative and quantitative data? • Are there opportunities for students to be universally screened? • Are there performance assessment options for students to demonstrate giftedness in the arts, creativity, and leadership? • Is there an opportunity to demonstrate outstanding performance through academic and/or talent portfolios? • Are language proficiency data reviewed for students demonstrating gifted potential throughout the school year? When and how often are data reviewed? • Is the option to use local norms available? • Are group-specific norm data available to use for either gifted identification or talent development opportunities?
Programming
• Are gifted _____ able to see and hear themselves in the curriculum? • How is heritage language intentionally valued and incorporated? • Do gifted _____ have access to advanced linguistic supports? • Are there opportunities for gifted _____ to develop critical and creative thinking?

Programming
• Are _____ students provided with authentic learning experiences that reflect their native culture? • What opportunities exist for gifted _____ to access advanced programming and acceleration throughout their school career? • What available grouping and pacing opportunities exist for advanced academic and social emotional needs? • How do gifted _____ participate in advanced programming options such as Advanced Placement, International Baccalaureate, and concurrent enrollment? • Are there talent development opportunities provided for gifted _____?
Professional learning
• Does your school district have a strategic plan for developing culturally responsive gifted professionals? • Are there professional learning opportunities for educators and administrators to explore and reflect upon their own cultural identity, including the role of microaggression and implicit bias? • How do educators and administrators actively learn about the values and cultures of their school and classroom community? • Are there gifted education professional learning opportunities for educators and administrators?
Family engagement
• How is information about gifted identification and advanced programming being communicated to _____ families? • Are _____ families being given multiple opportunities and ways to engage in conversations with teachers and administrators about their child? Are these conversations asset based? • In what ways are _____ families engaged in the school community? • In what ways is the school inviting _____ families in? • How does the school recognize and incorporate the strengths of _____ families into the classroom? • Is there a partnership with _____ families and teachers to promote the education of the child?

From Michelle Pacheco DuBois and Robin M. Greene, *Supporting gifted ELLs in the Latinx community: Practical strategies, K–12*. New York: Routledge. © 2021.

Made in United States
Orlando, FL
05 June 2023